I0468623

COLORING ART
BOOK 1
COLORING BOOK FOR BIG KIDS

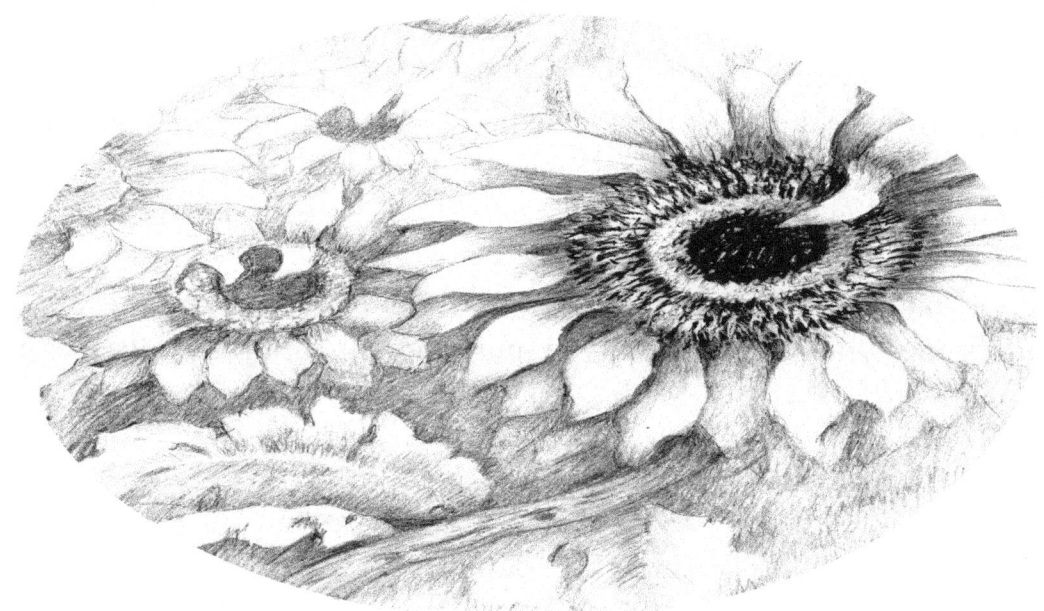

FUN FOR ALL AGES

63 BLACK & WHITE
ILLUSTRATIONS

PENNY & MIKE MAIER

PUBLISHED BY
AKASHIC SPIRIT PUBLISHING, LLC
DeFuniak Springs, FL

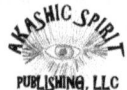

copyright©2016 Penny Maier

Penny and Mike have collected these drawings from sketch books created by: Lee K. (1928-2015). She has passed away, but the beauty she produced can give pleasure to those who choose to add their talents by filling in colors of their choice. Most of these drawings were not signed, so assigning an artist to the drawing is problematic. Lee K. was inclined to sign them, so you will see her signature in a few of the sketches. Many of the sketches were edited to fit this platform.

Passing the time coloring in these drawing can have the effect of meditation; allowing your mind to relax and following your colorful intuition. Please, have fun by coloring in the drawings with color pencils, markers or pastels.

A special note to those who want to use markers, place a backup sheet to catch the bleed through. If you use pastels, you must know about the smudge factor.

http://www.akashicspiritualcenter.org

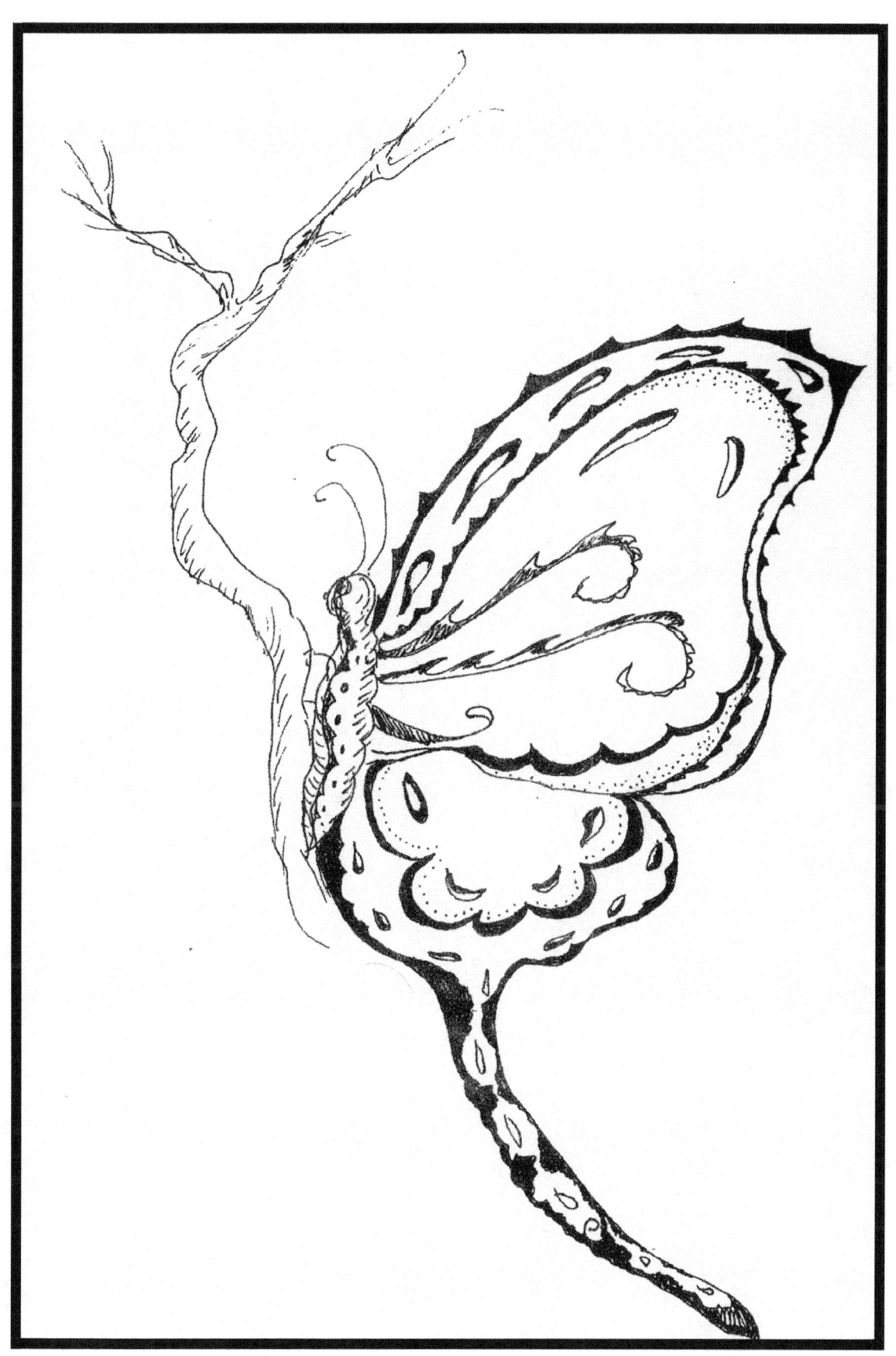

COLORING ART (COLORING BOOK FOR BIG KIDS) BOOK 1

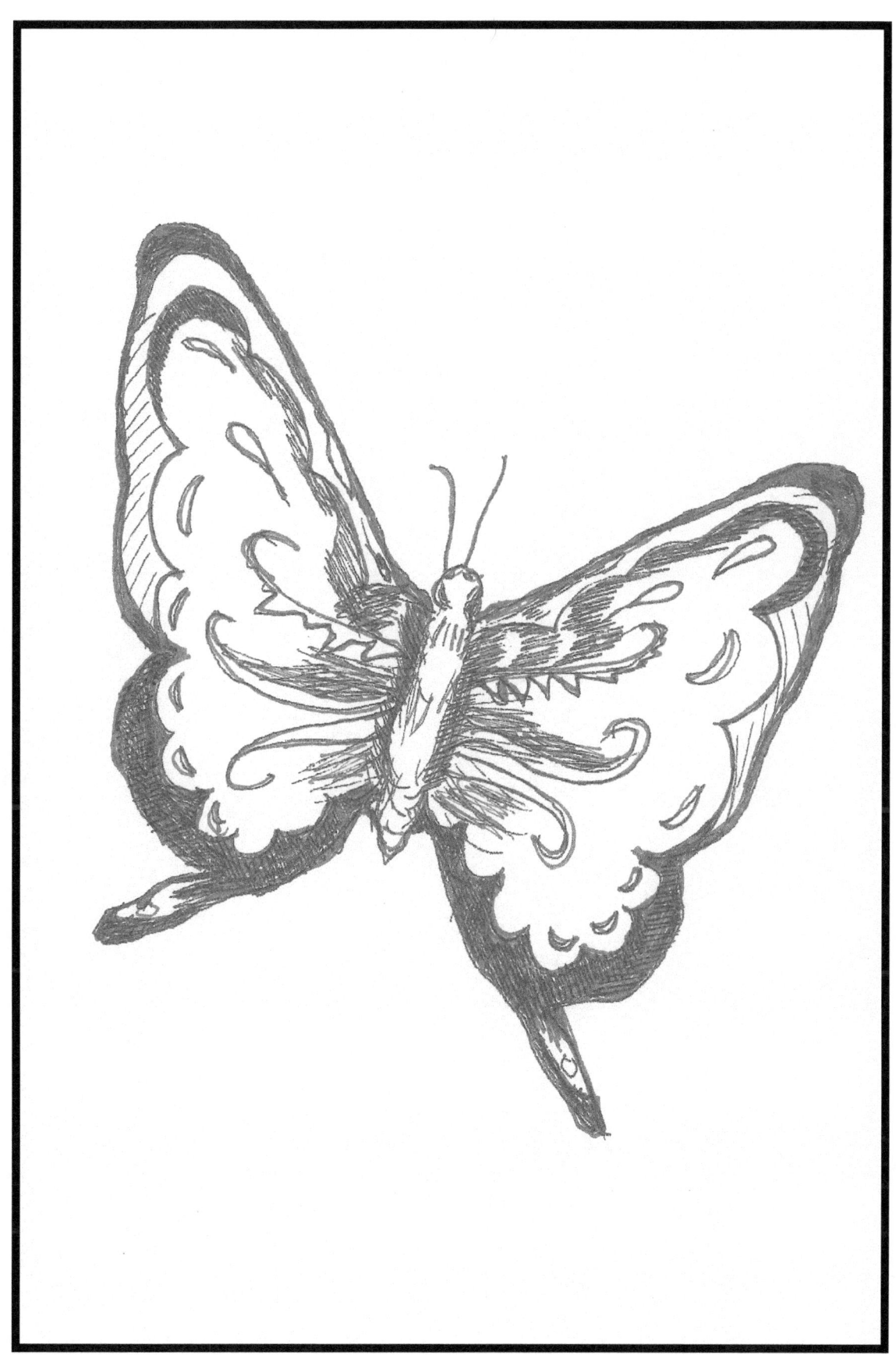

COLORING ART (COLORING BOOK FOR BIG KIDS) BOOK 1

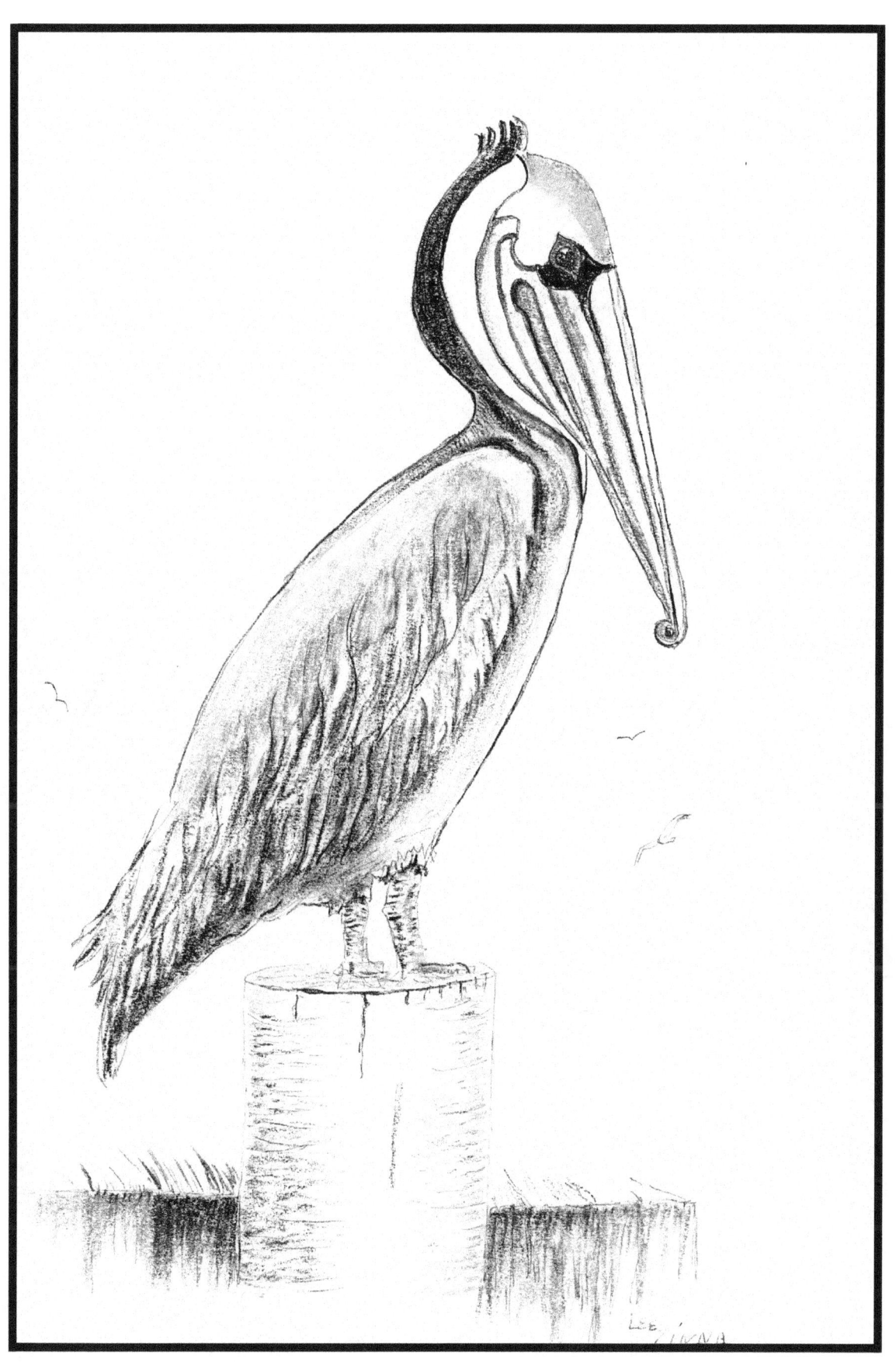

COLORING ART (COLORING BOOK FOR BIG KIDS) BOOK 1

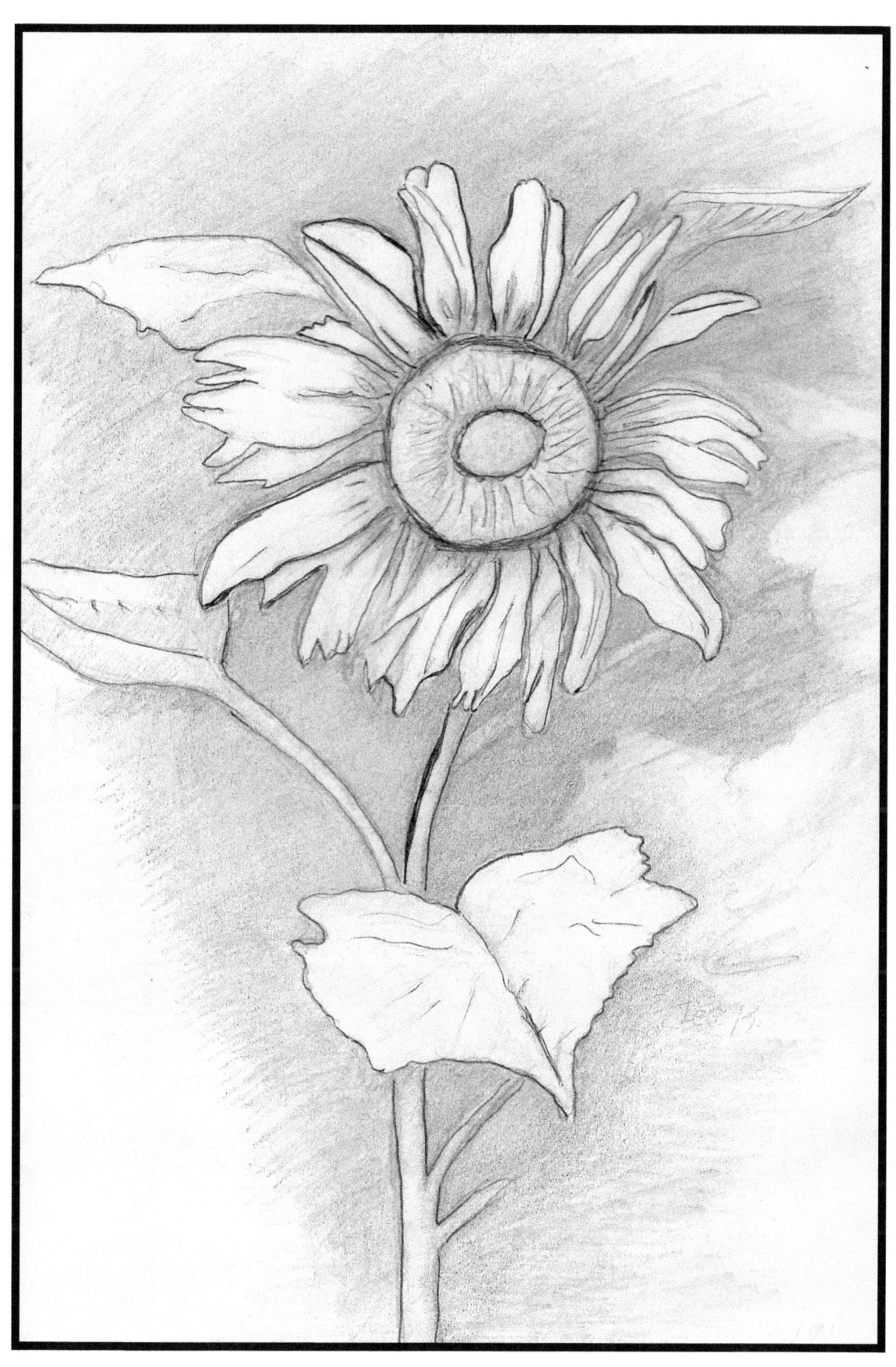

COLORING ART (COLORING BOOK FOR BIG KIDS) BOOK 1

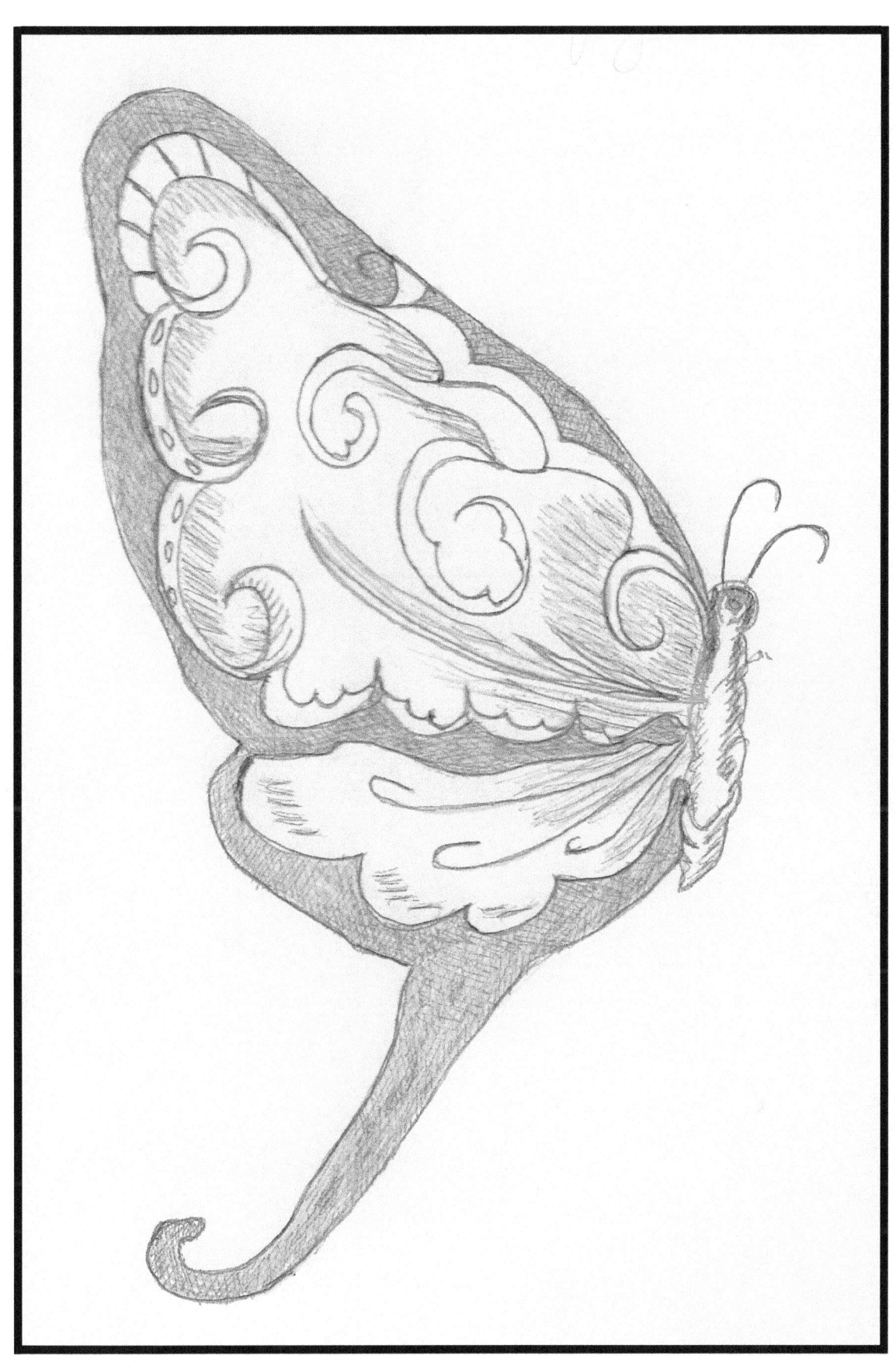

COLORING ART (COLORING BOOK FOR BIG KIDS) BOOK 1

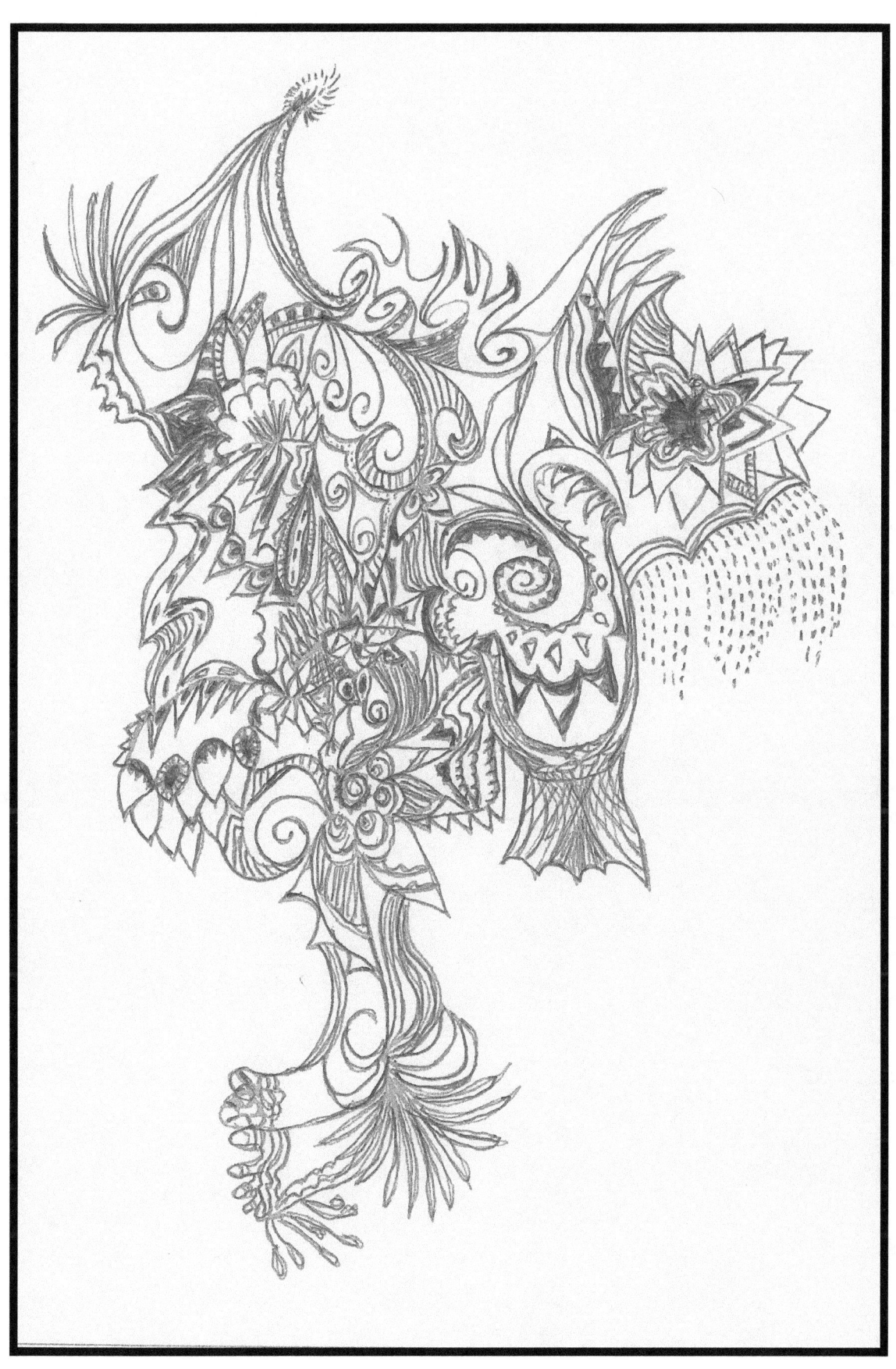

COLORING ART (COLORING BOOK FOR BIG KIDS) BOOK 1

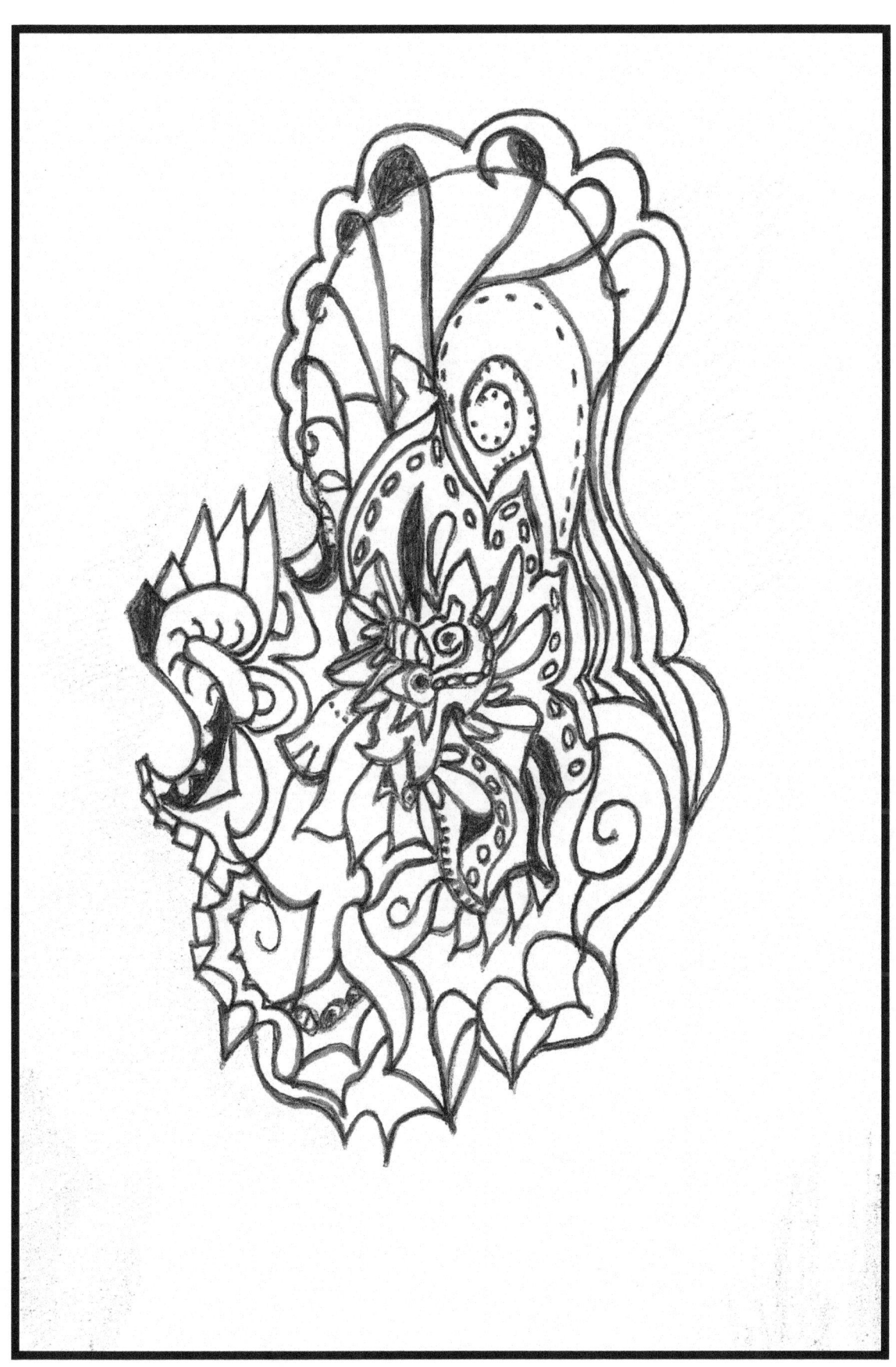

COLORING ART (COLORING BOOK FOR BIG KIDS) BOOK 1

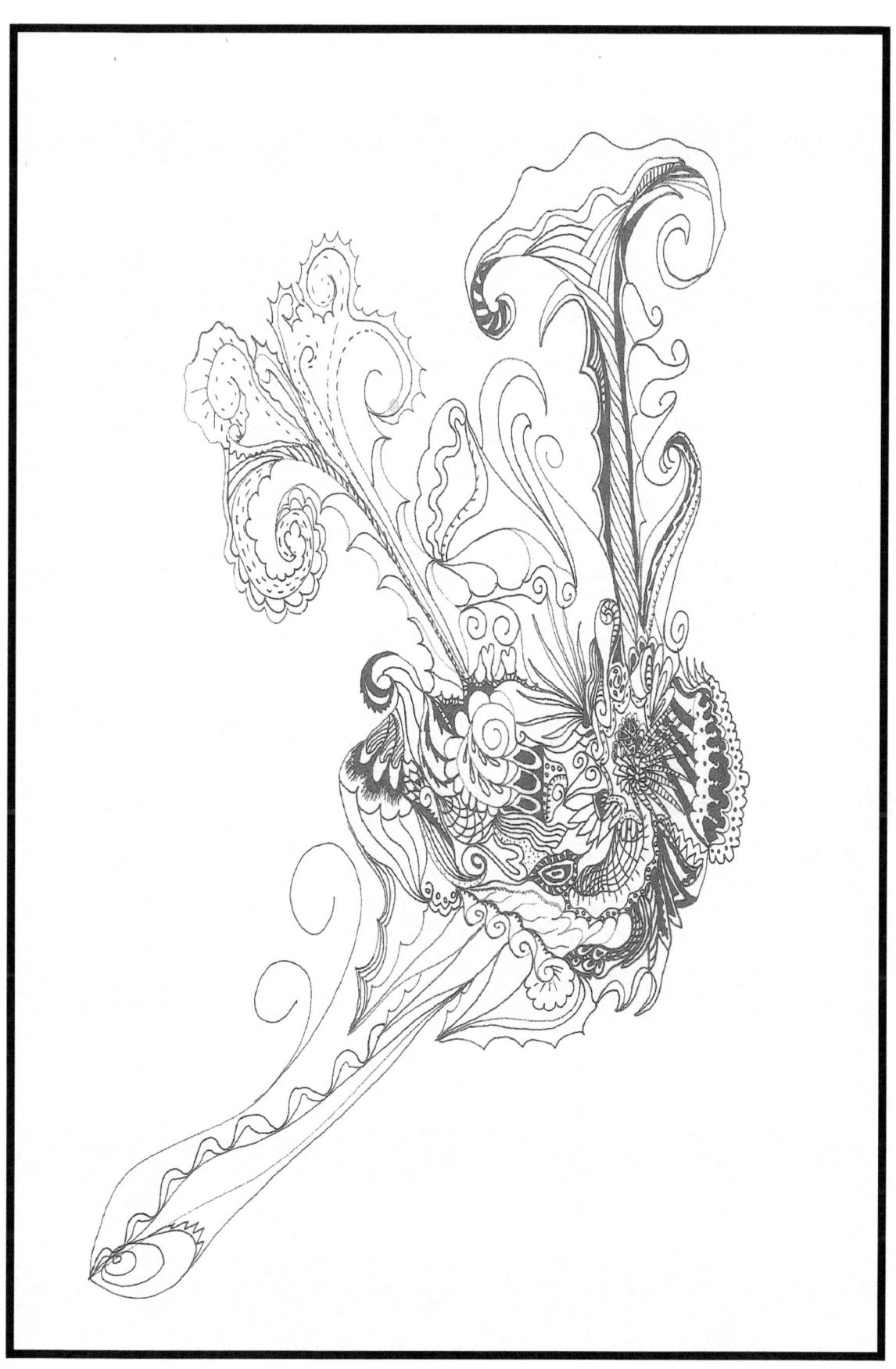

COLORING ART (COLORING BOOK FOR BIG KIDS) BOOK 1

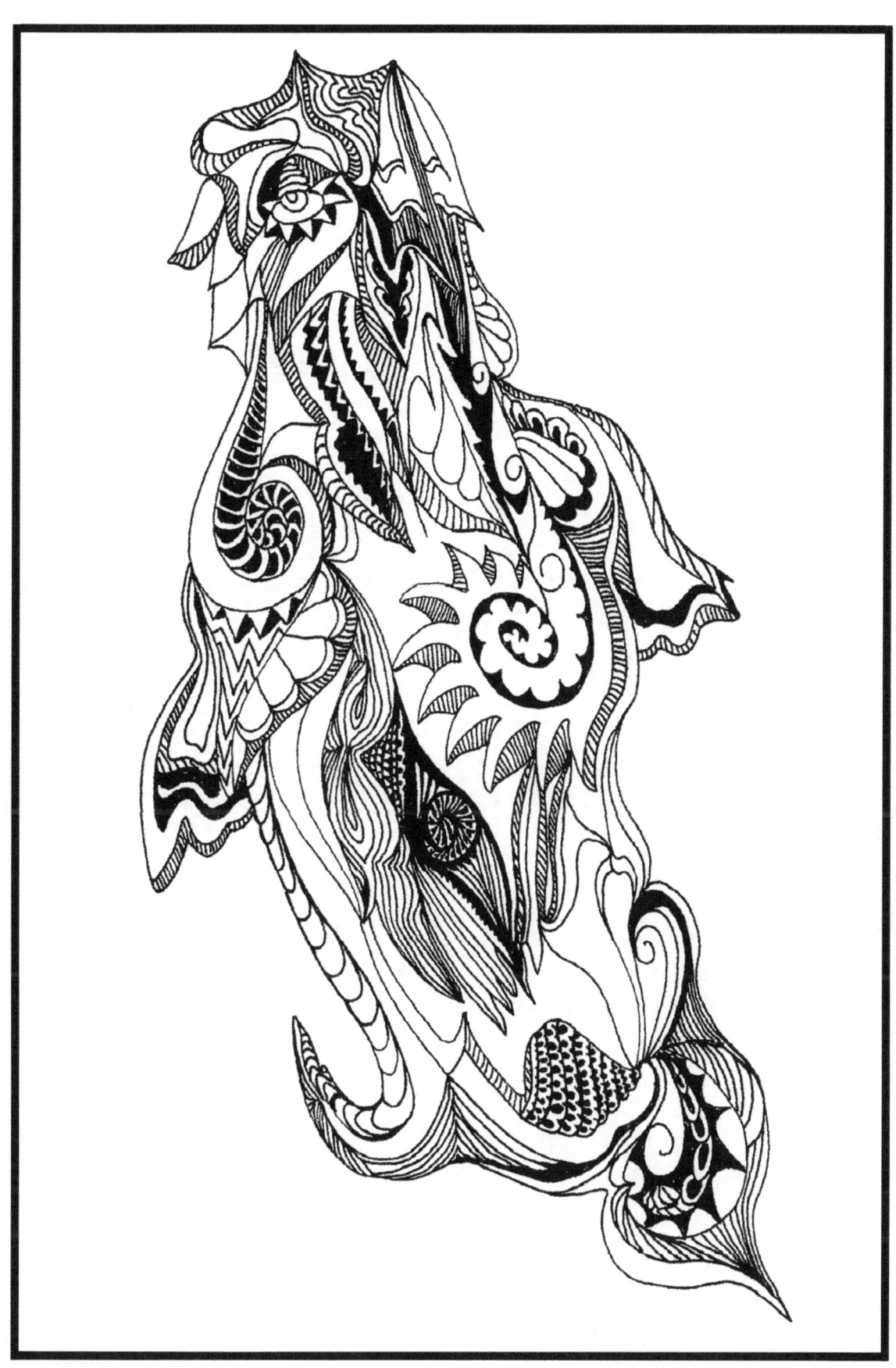

COLORING ART (COLORING BOOK FOR BIG KIDS) BOOK 1

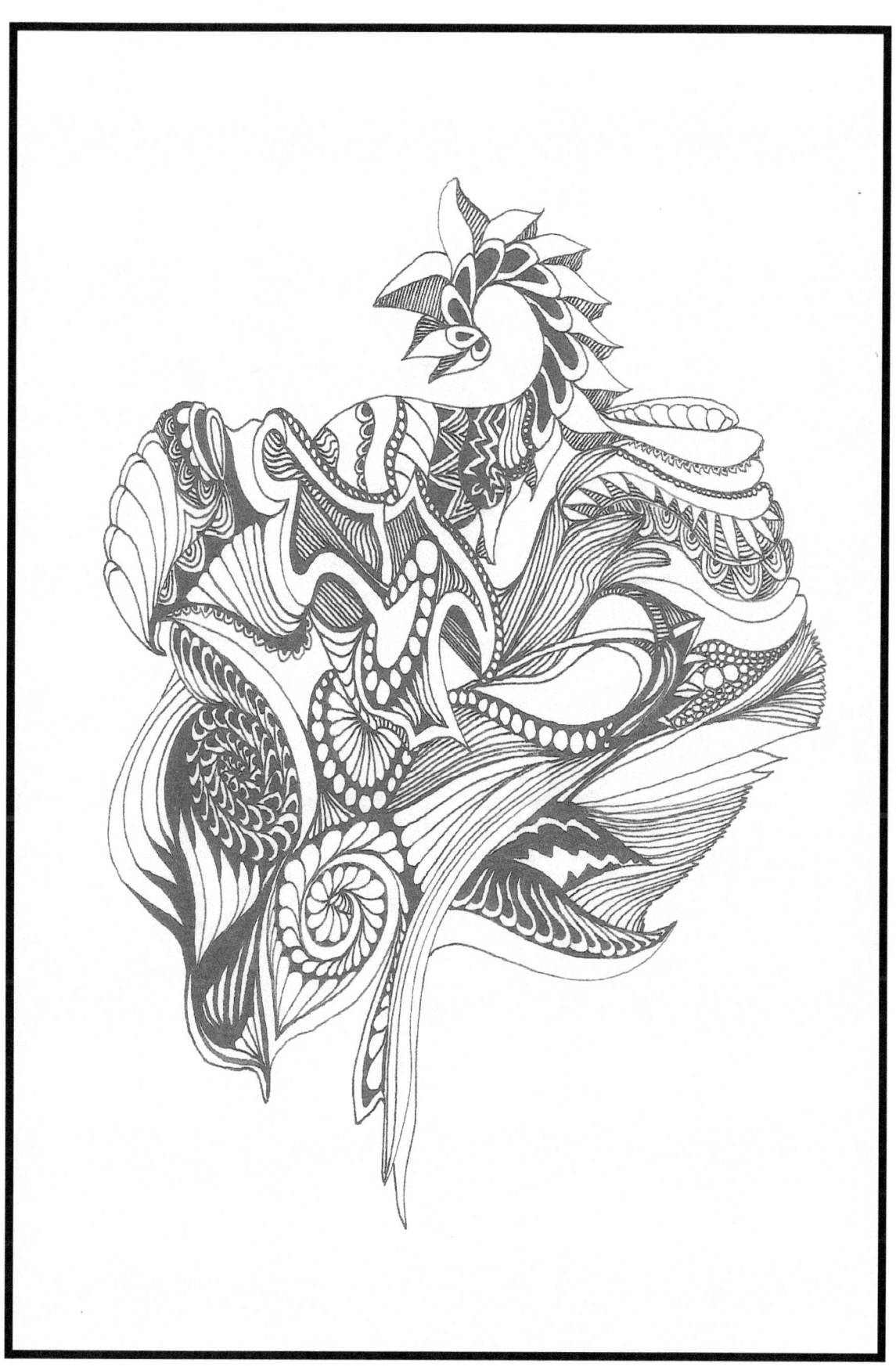

COLORING ART (COLORING BOOK FOR BIG KIDS) BOOK 1

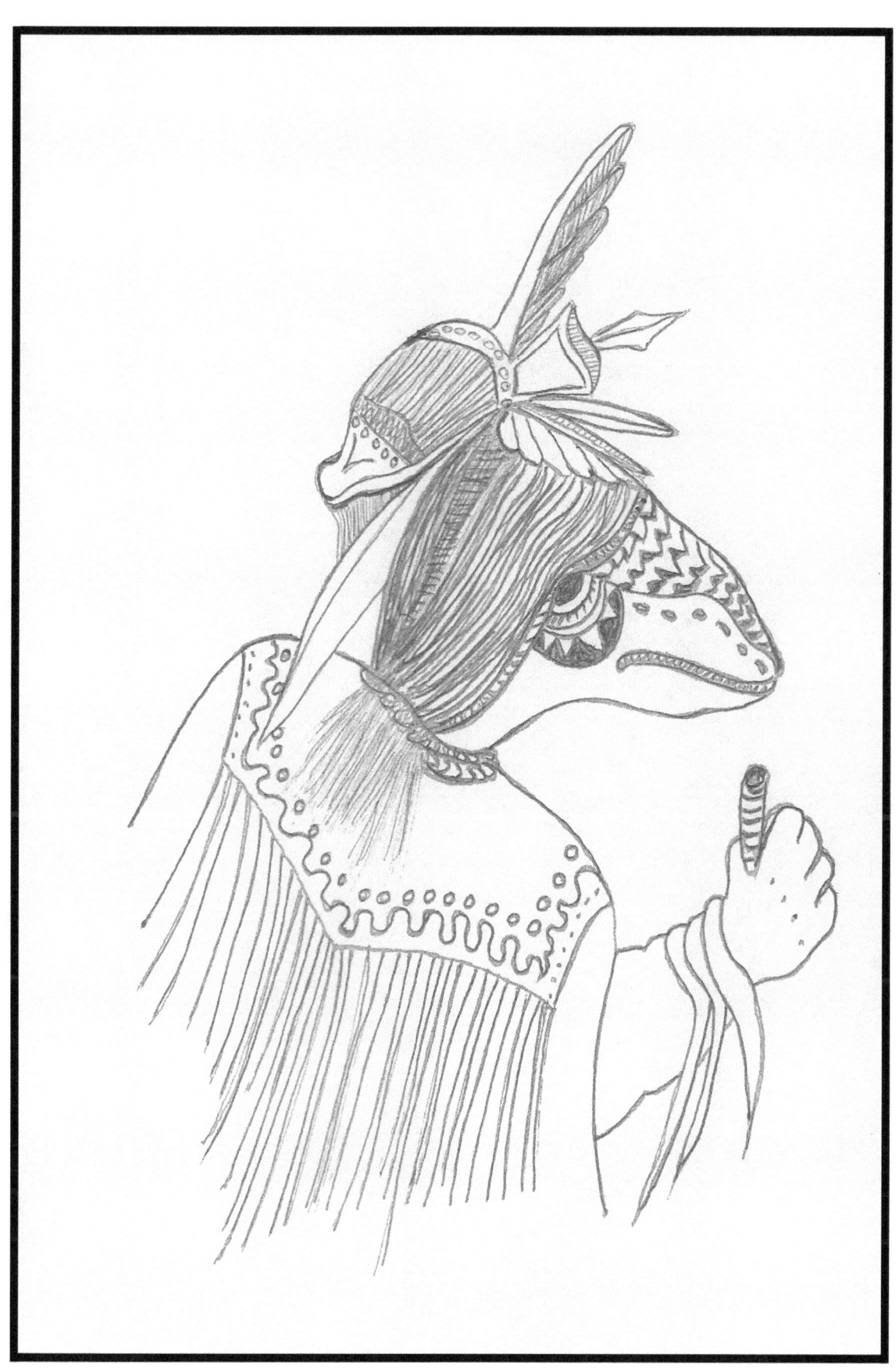

COLORING ART (COLORING BOOK FOR BIG KIDS) BOOK 1

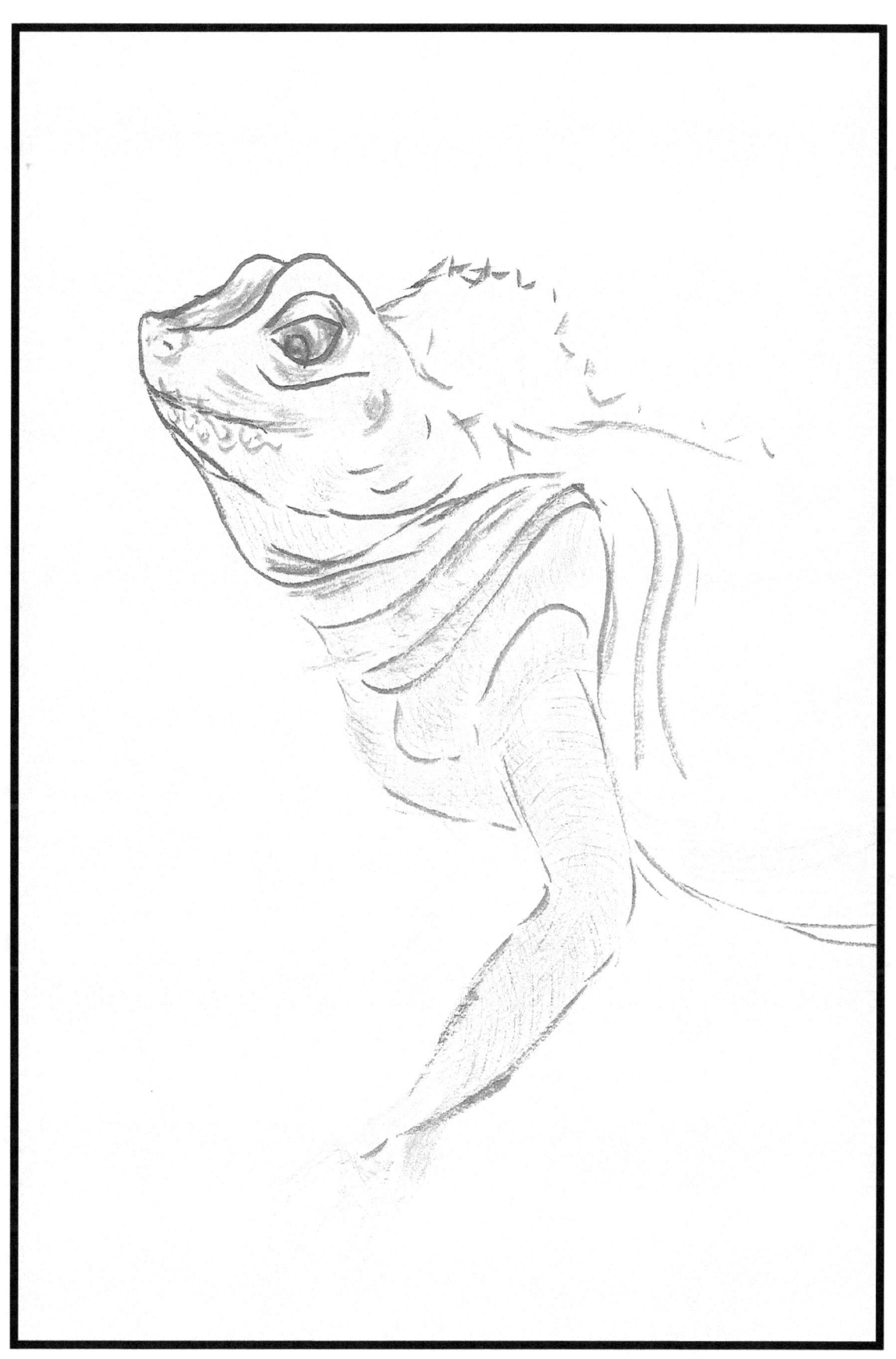

COLORING ART (COLORING BOOK FOR BIG KIDS) BOOK 1

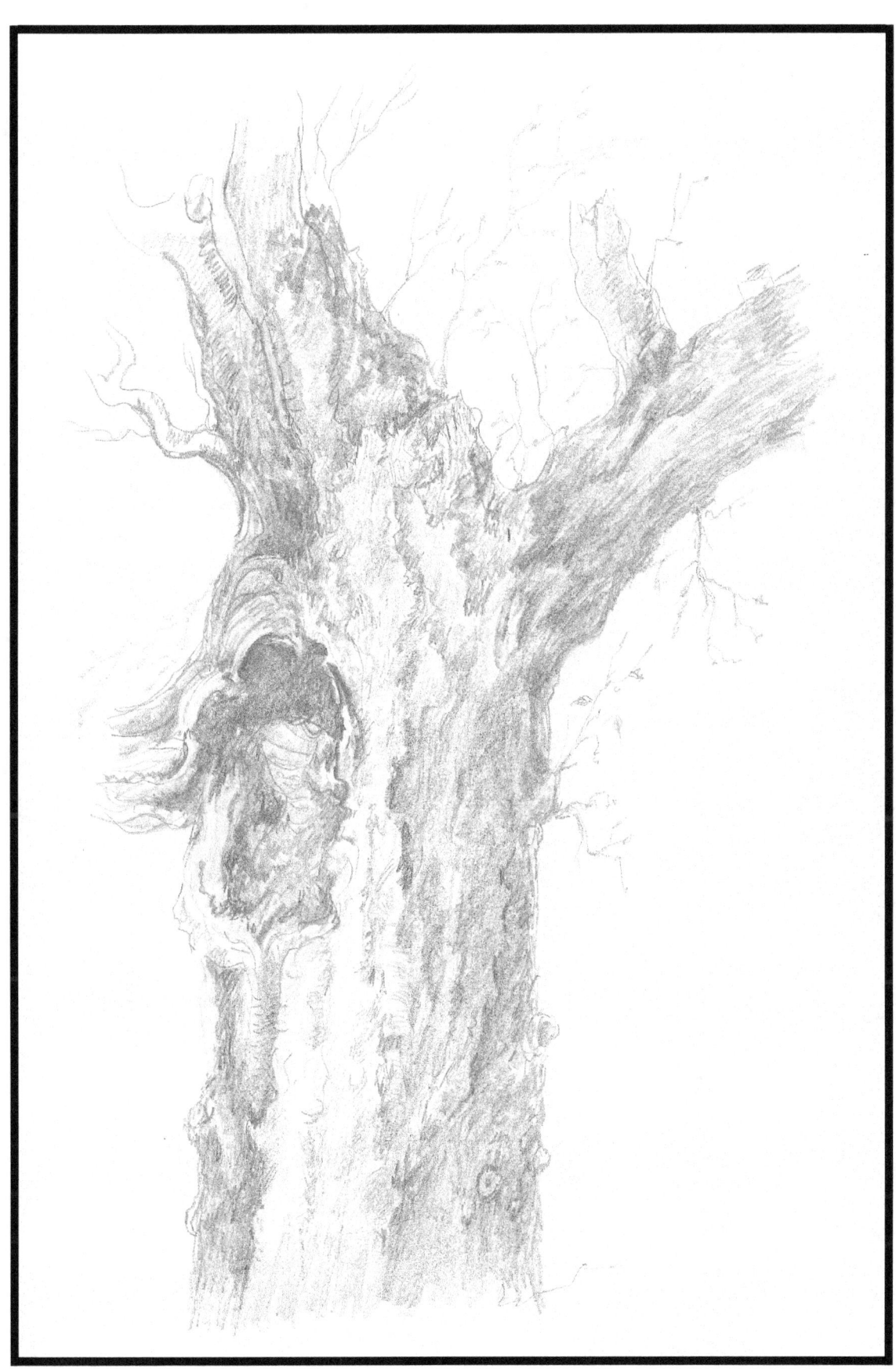

COLORING ART (COLORING BOOK FOR BIG KIDS) BOOK 1

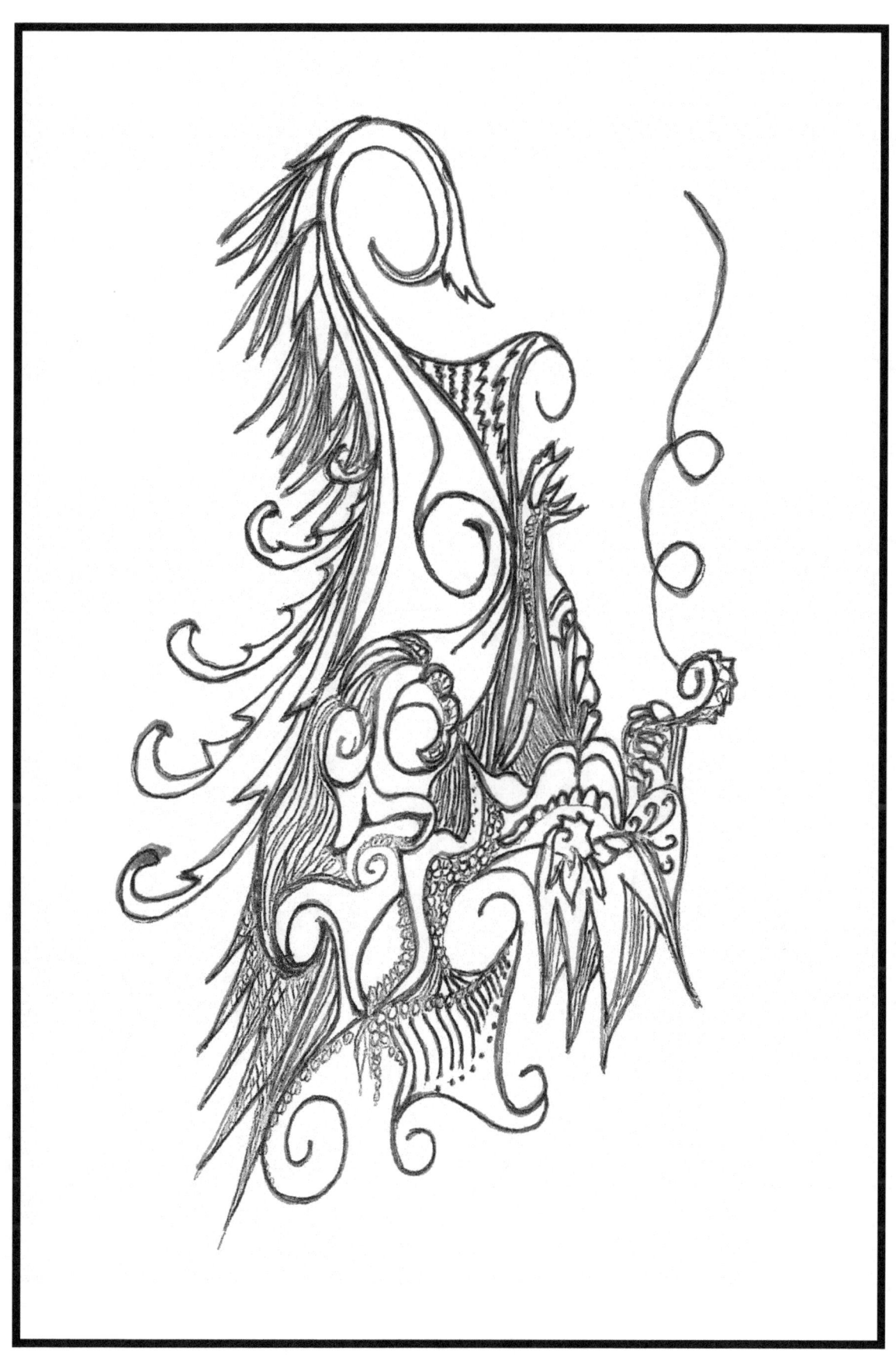

COLORING ART (COLORING BOOK FOR BIG KIDS) BOOK 1

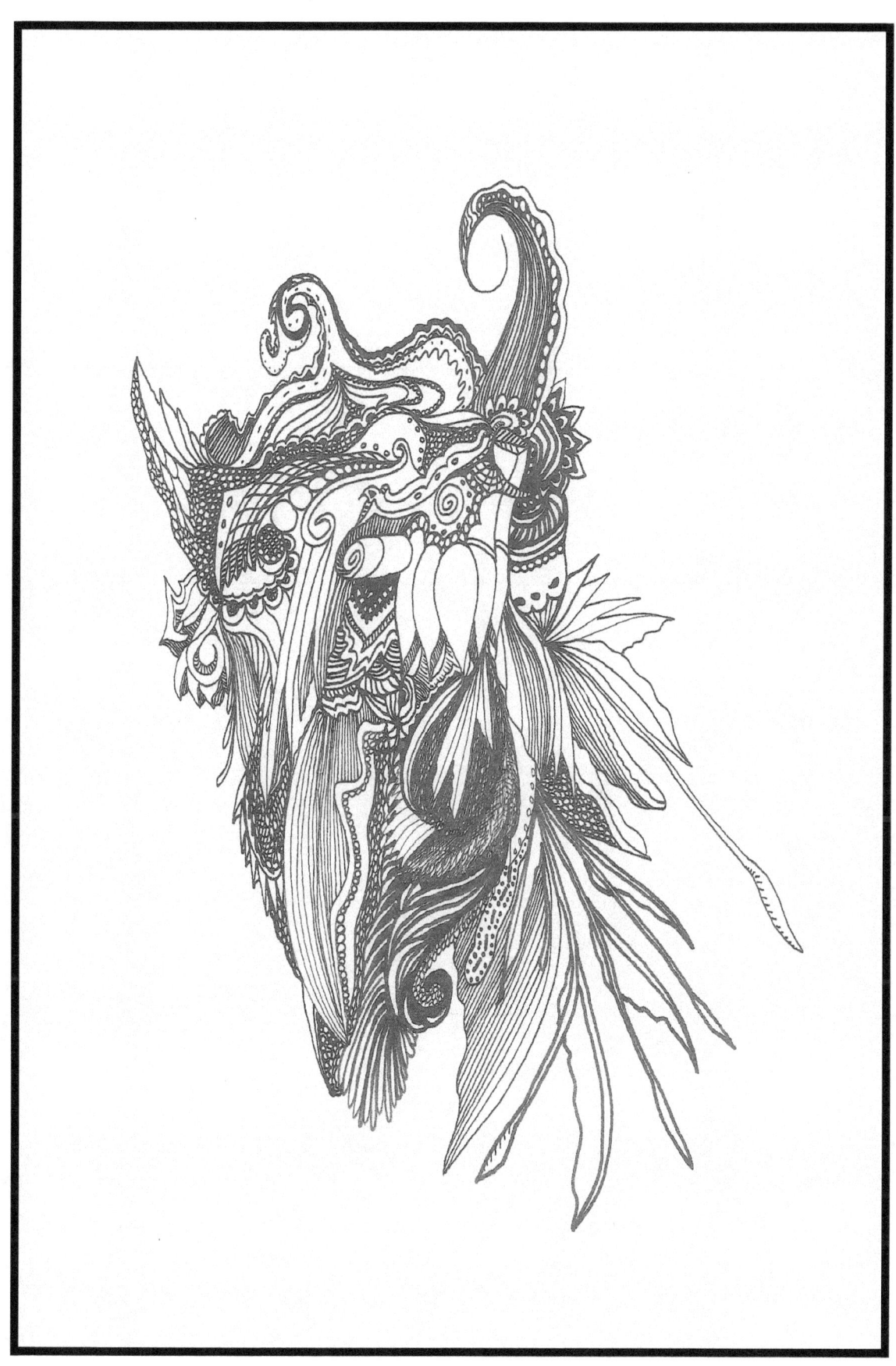

COLORING ART (COLORING BOOK FOR BIG KIDS) BOOK 1

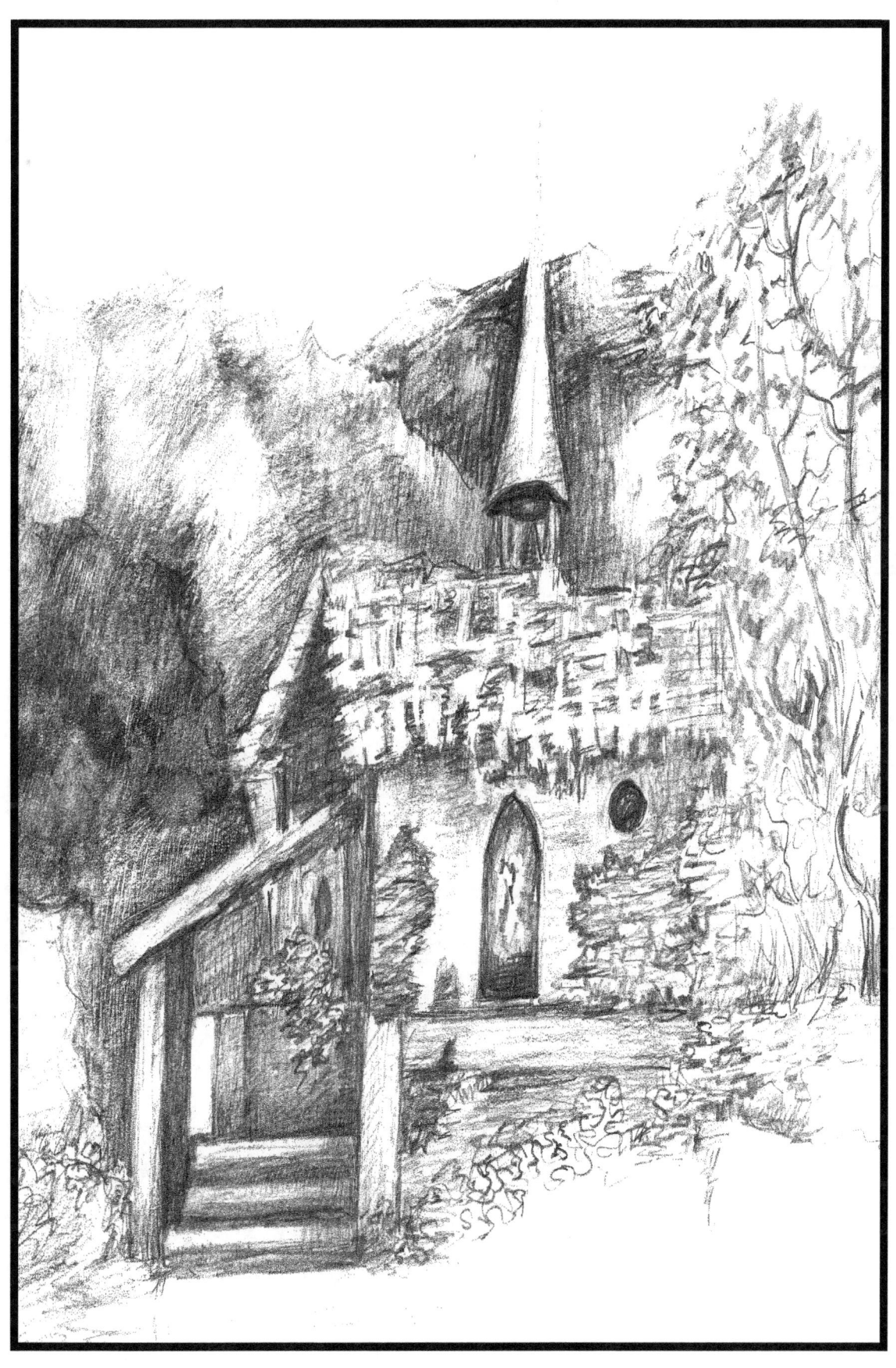

COLORING ART (COLORING BOOK FOR BIG KIDS) BOOK 1

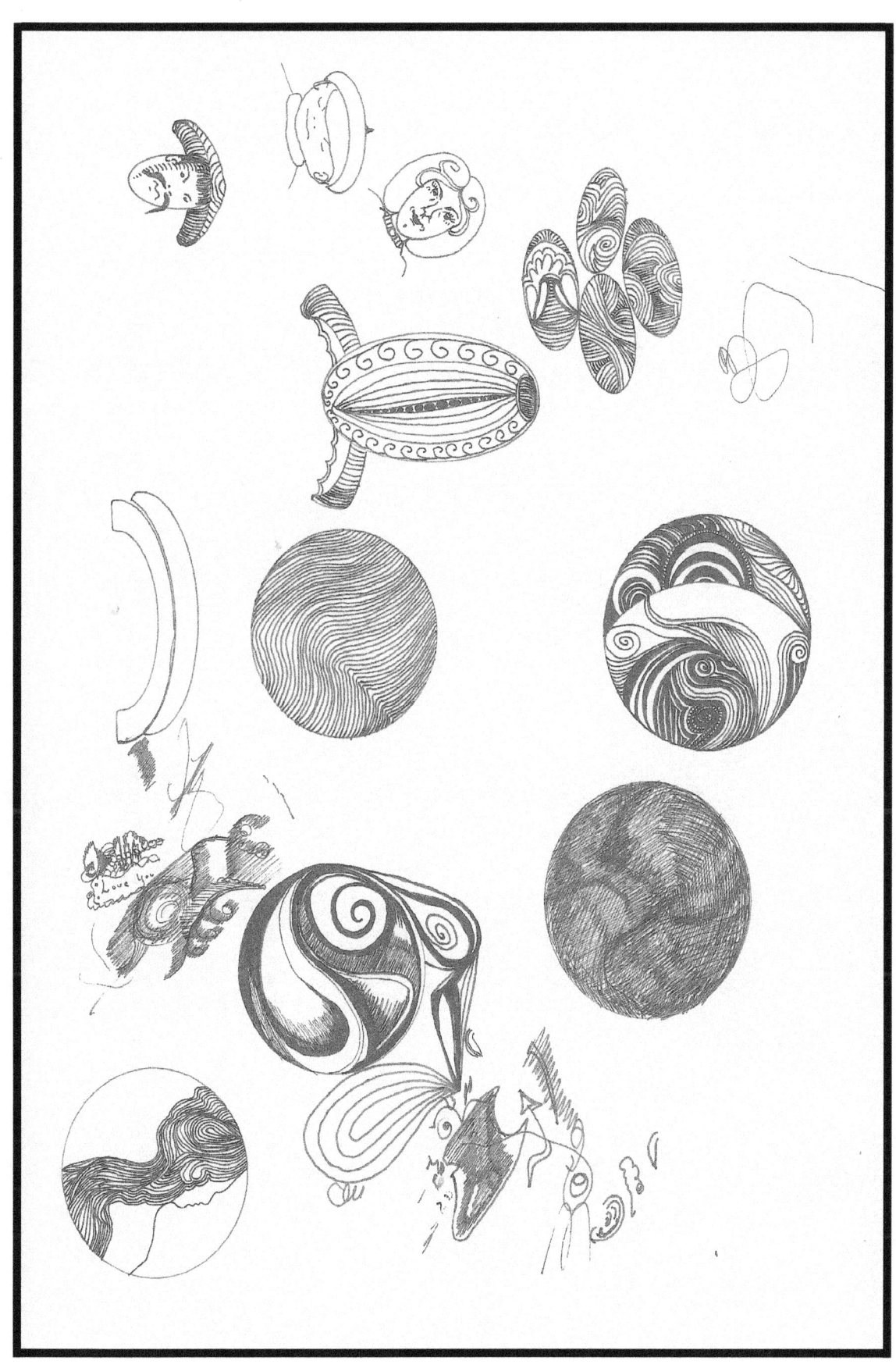

COLORING ART (COLORING BOOK FOR BIG KIDS) BOOK 1

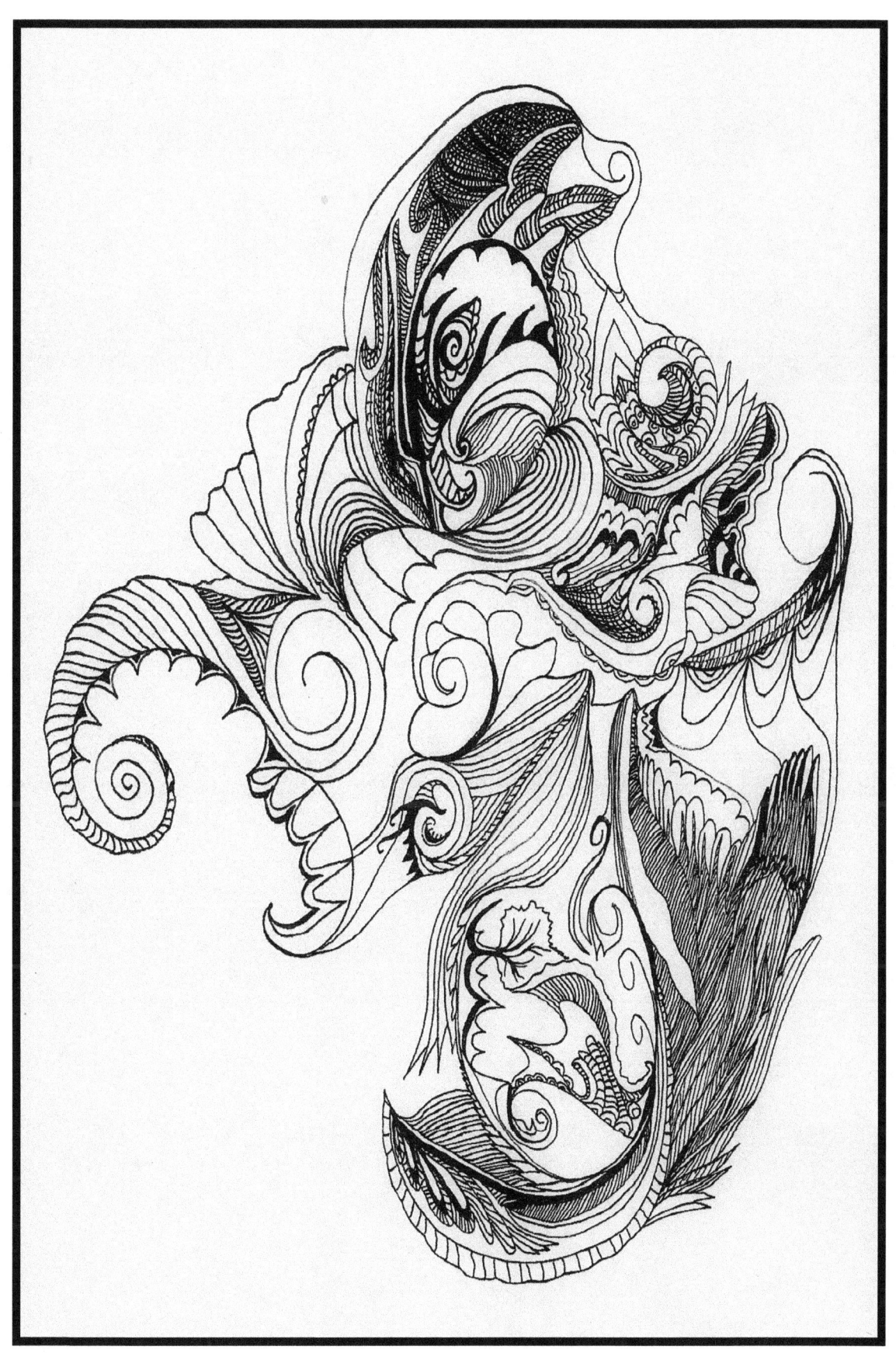

COLORING ART (COLORING BOOK FOR BIG KIDS) BOOK 1

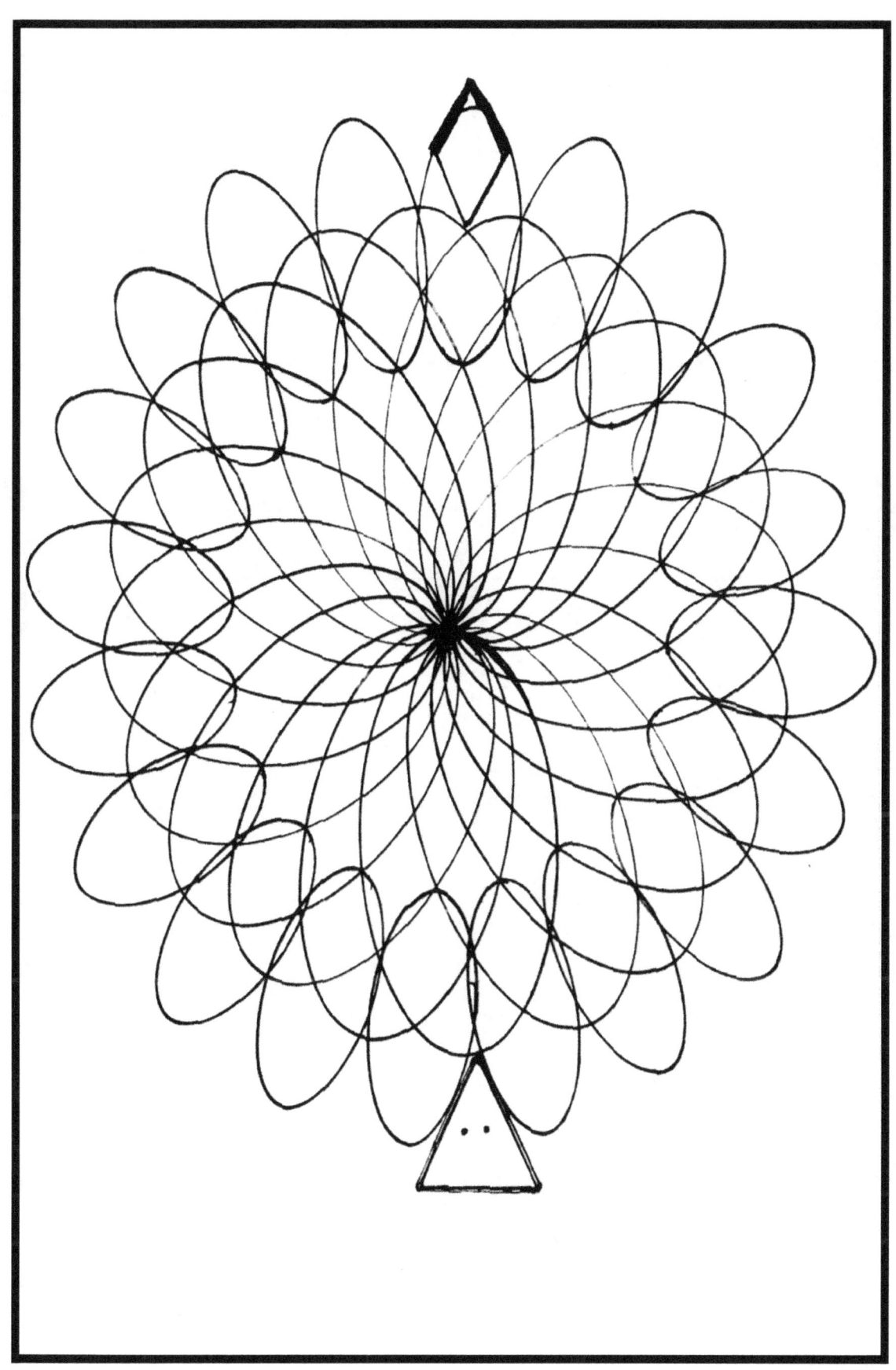

COLORING ART (COLORING BOOK FOR BIG KIDS) BOOK 1

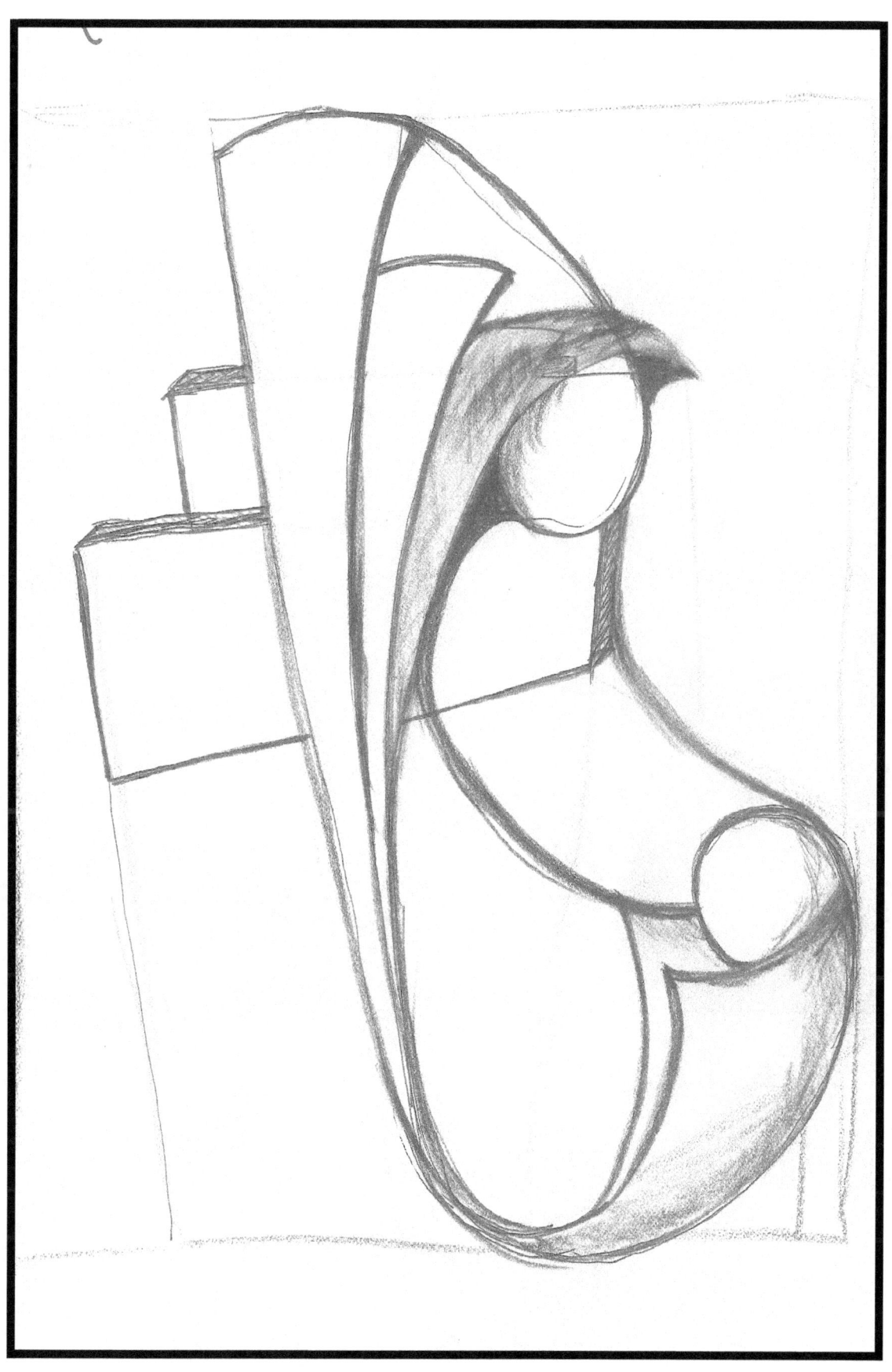

COLORING ART (COLORING BOOK FOR BIG KIDS) BOOK 1

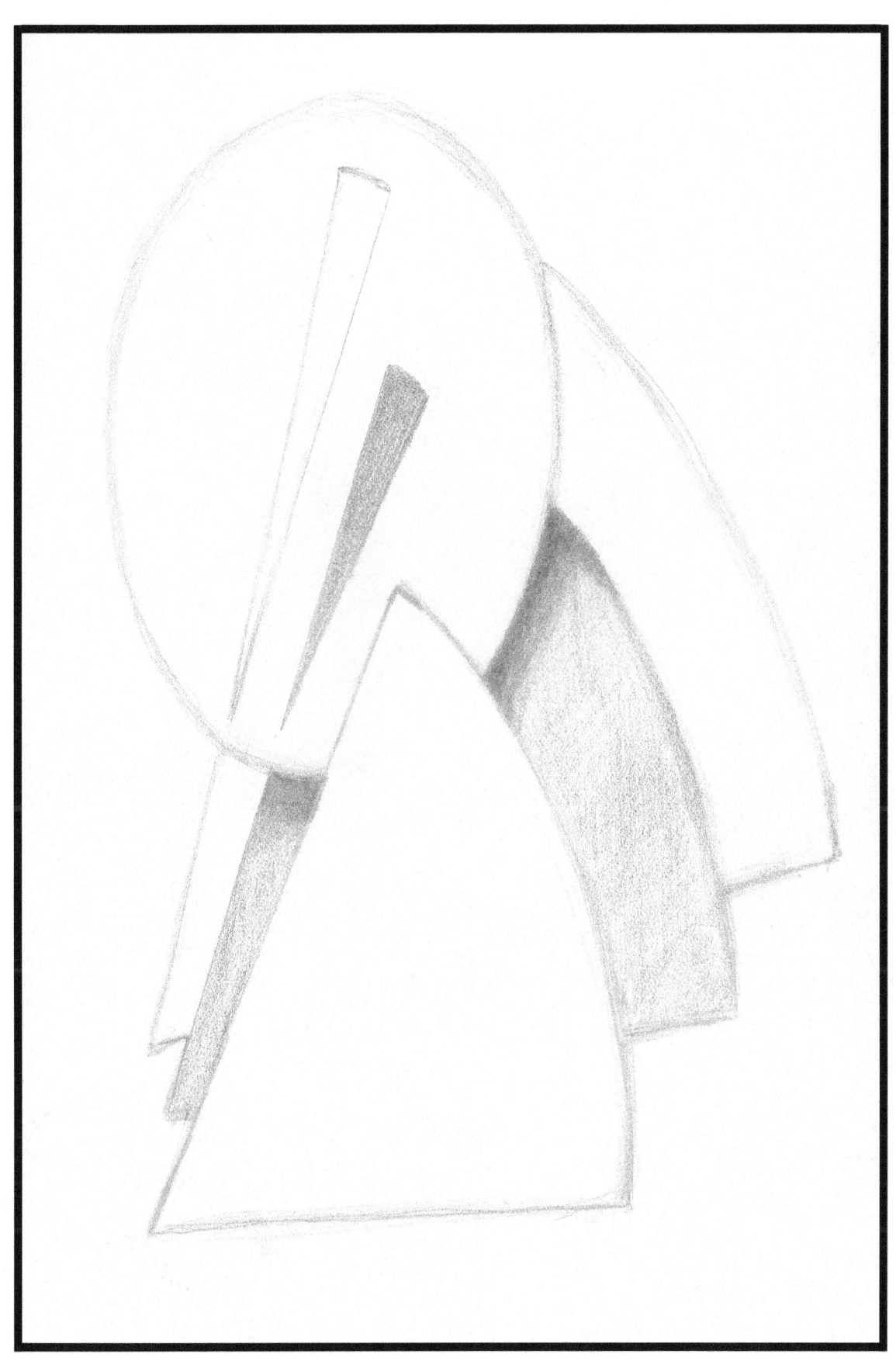

COLORING ART (COLORING BOOK FOR BIG KIDS) BOOK 1

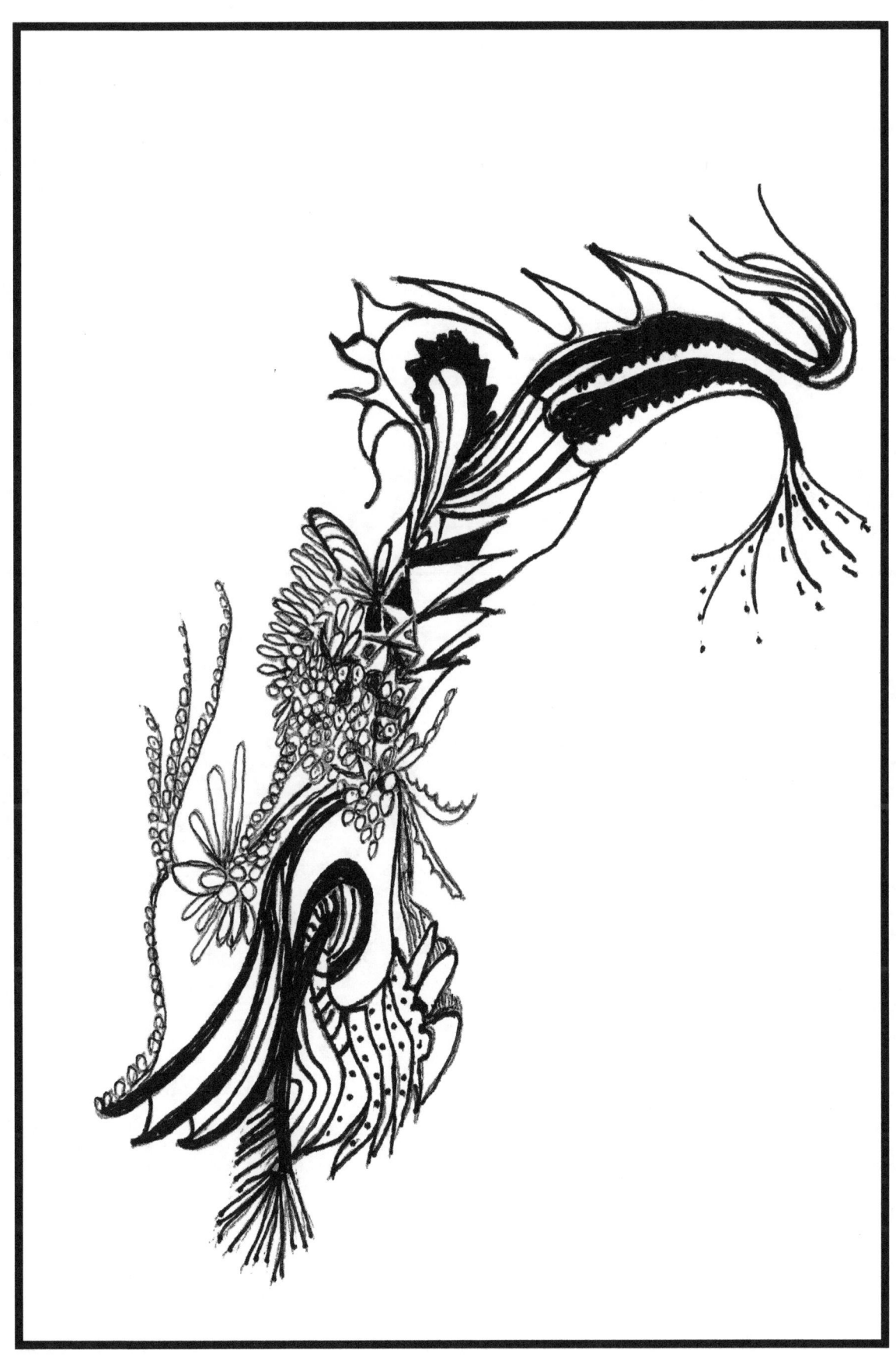

COLORING ART (COLORING BOOK FOR BIG KIDS) BOOK 1

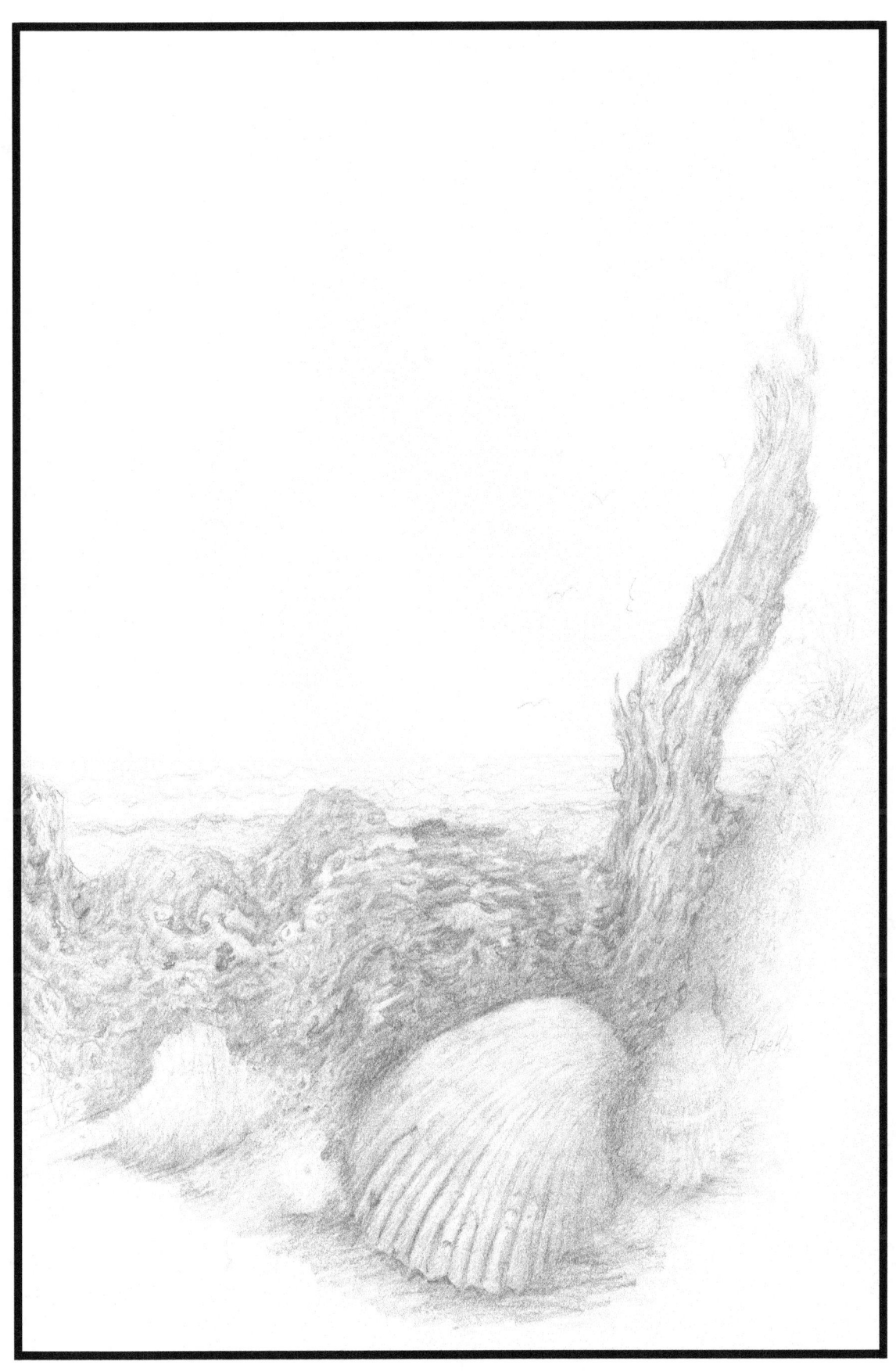

COLORING ART (COLORING BOOK FOR BIG KIDS) BOOK 1

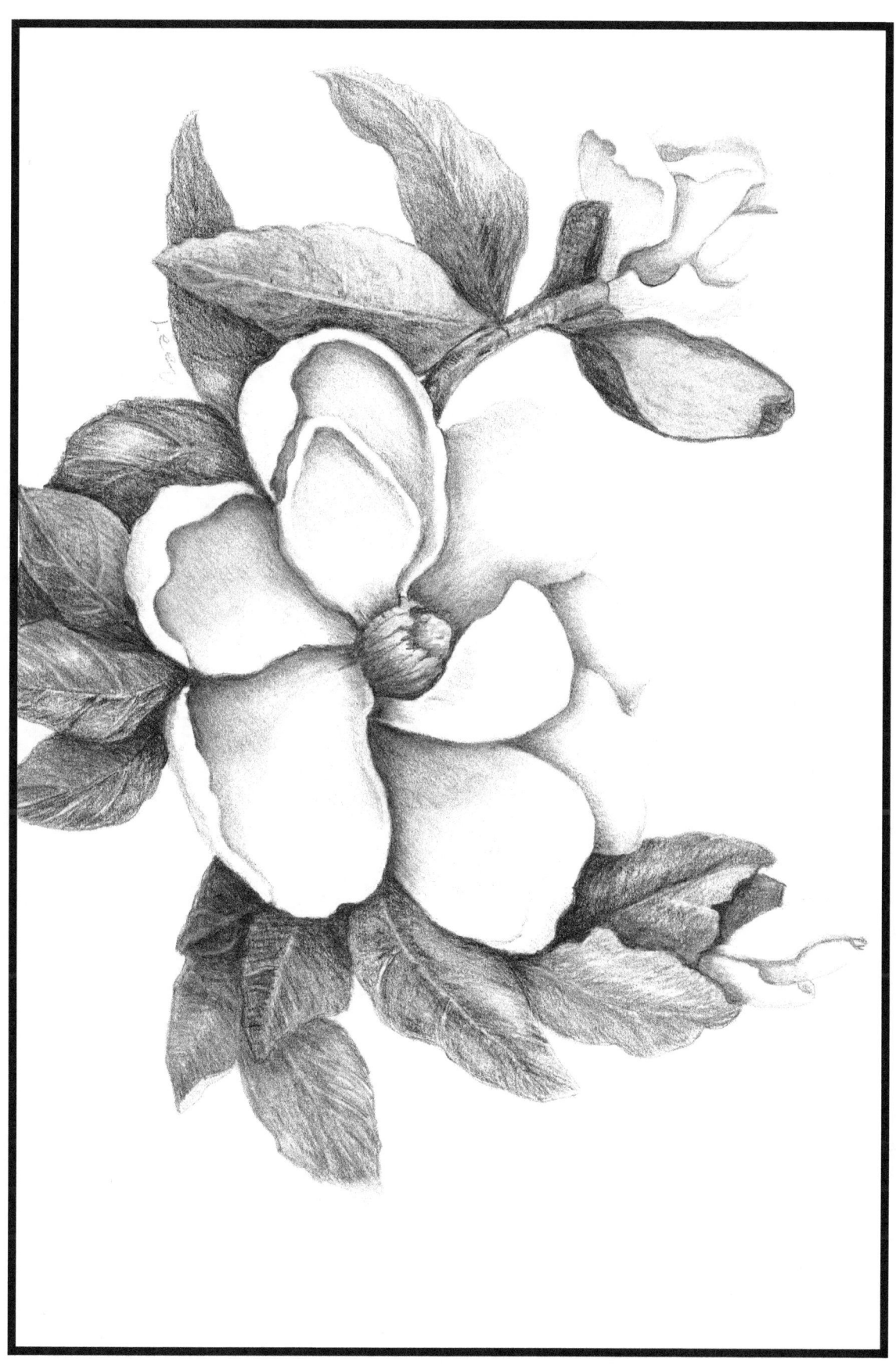

COLORING ART (COLORING BOOK FOR BIG KIDS) BOOK 1

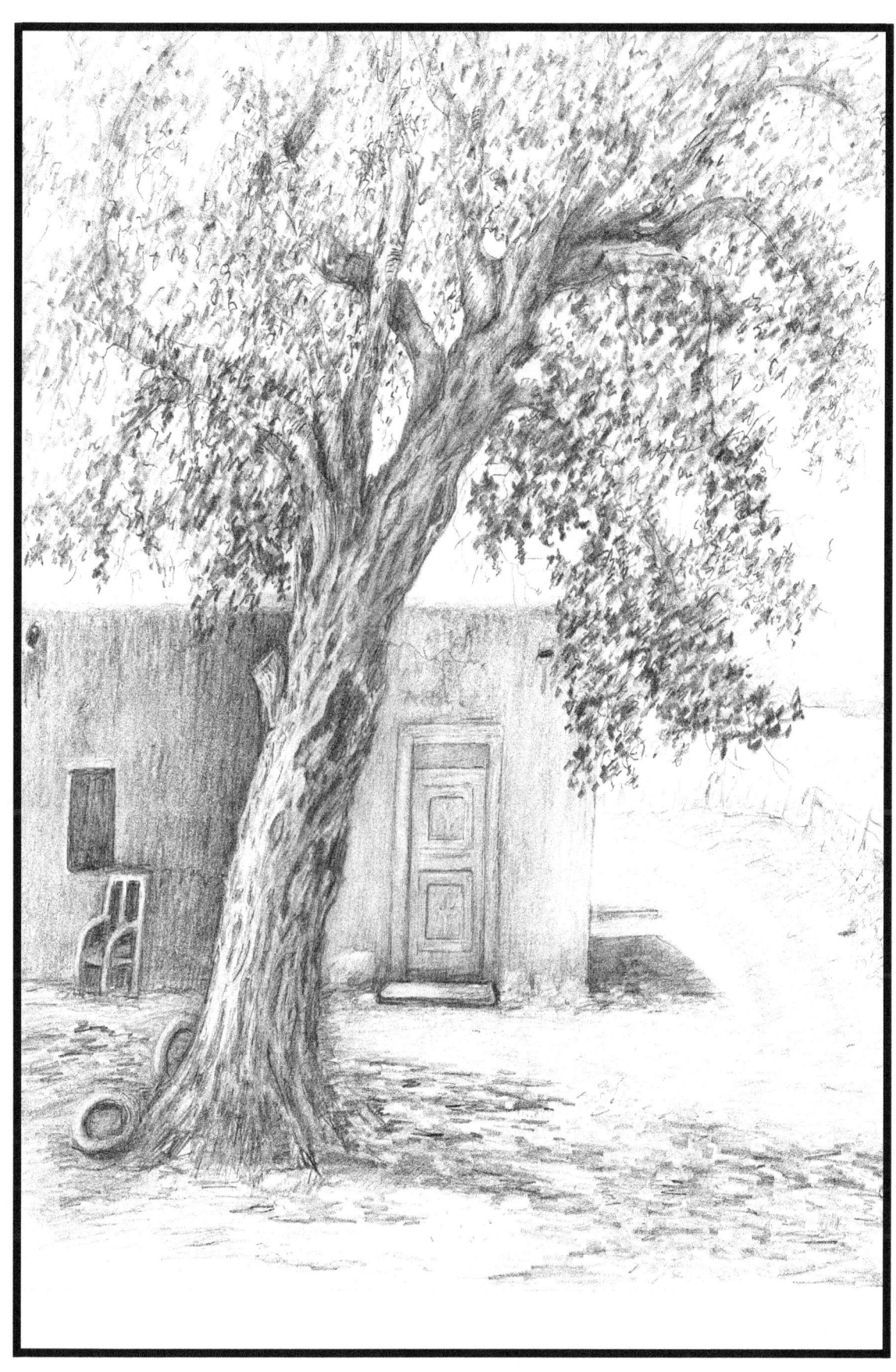

COLORING ART (COLORING BOOK FOR BIG KIDS) BOOK 1

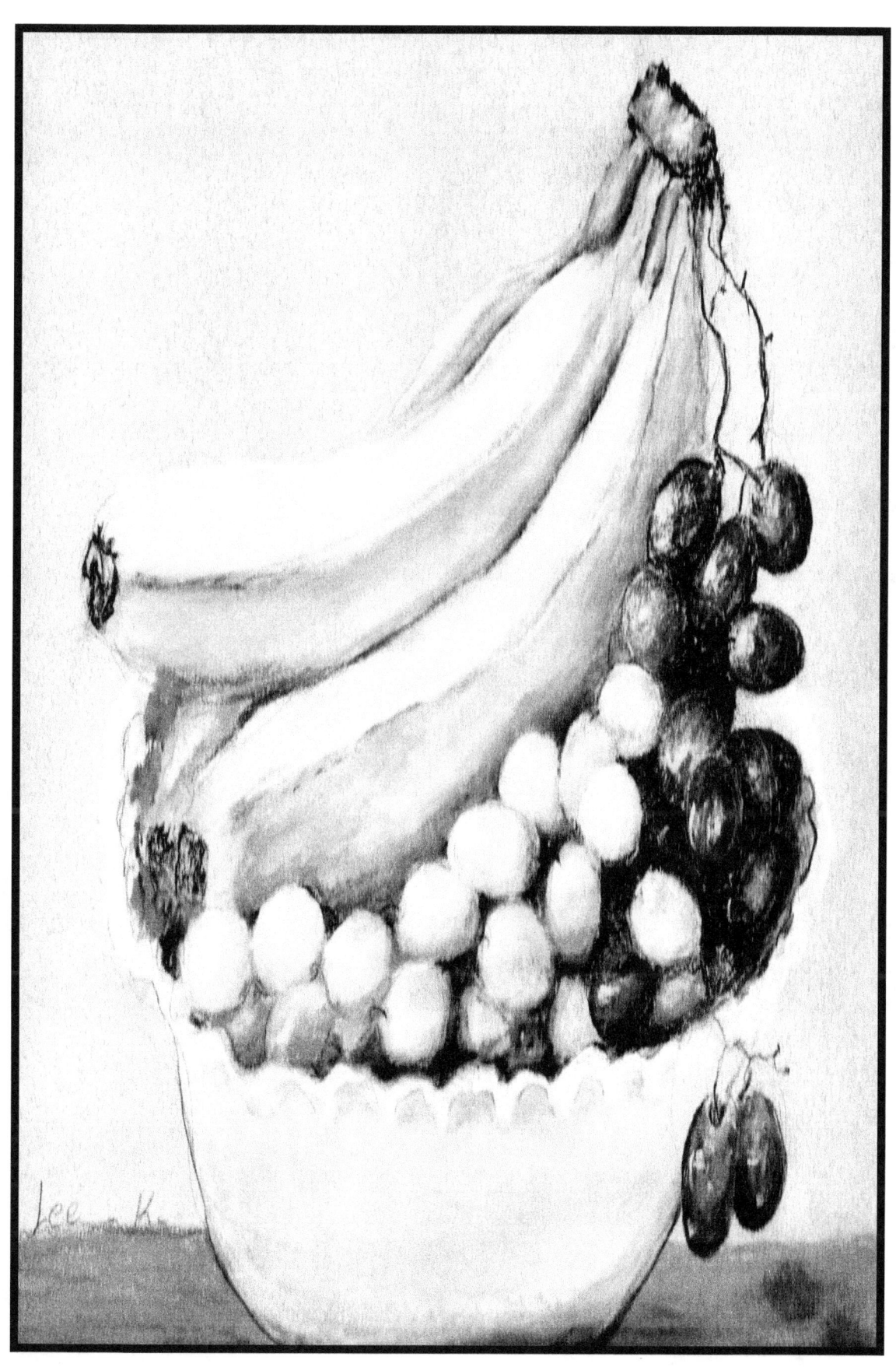

COLORING ART (COLORING BOOK FOR BIG KIDS) BOOK 1

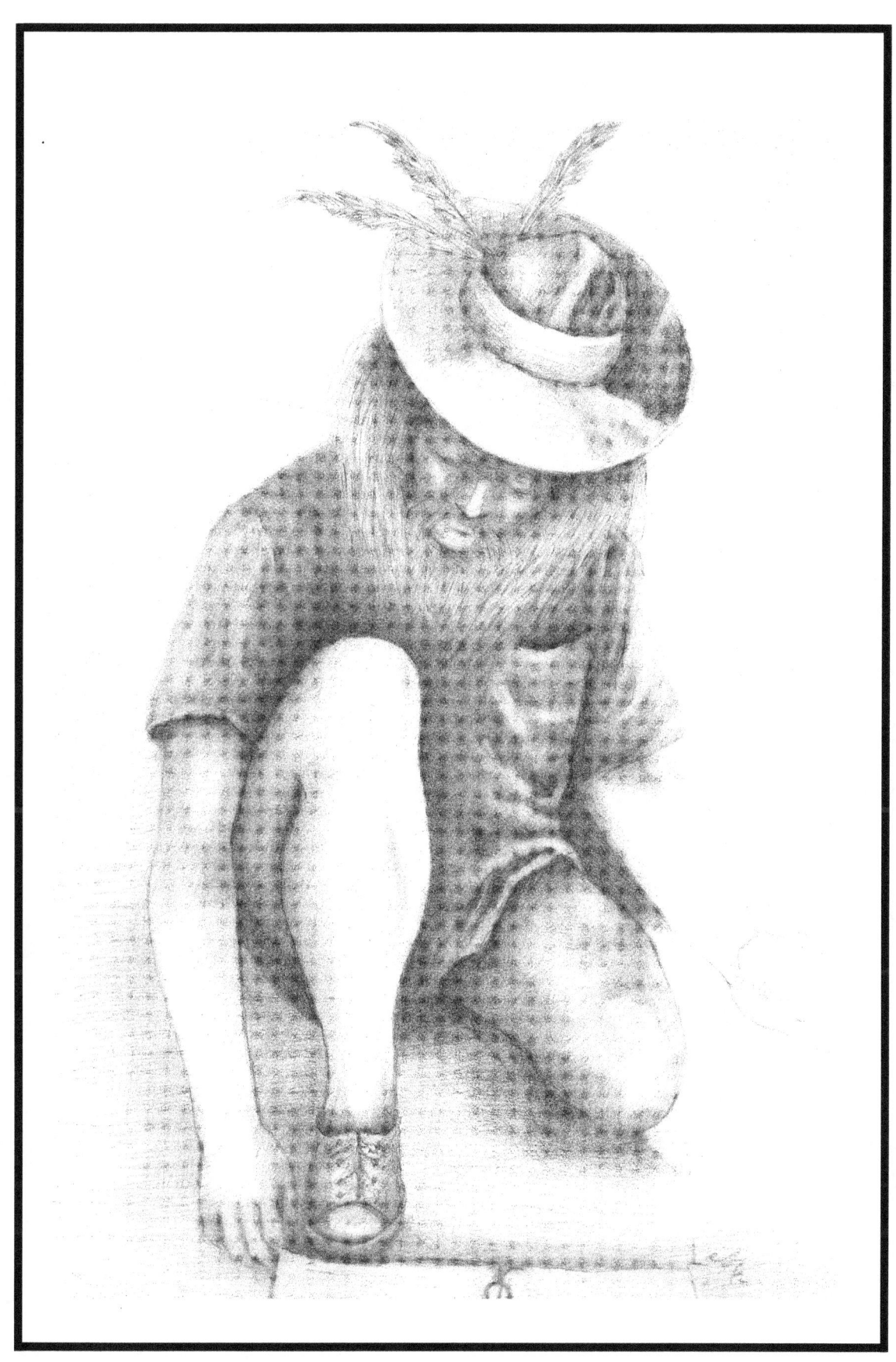

COLORING ART (COLORING BOOK FOR BIG KIDS) BOOK 1

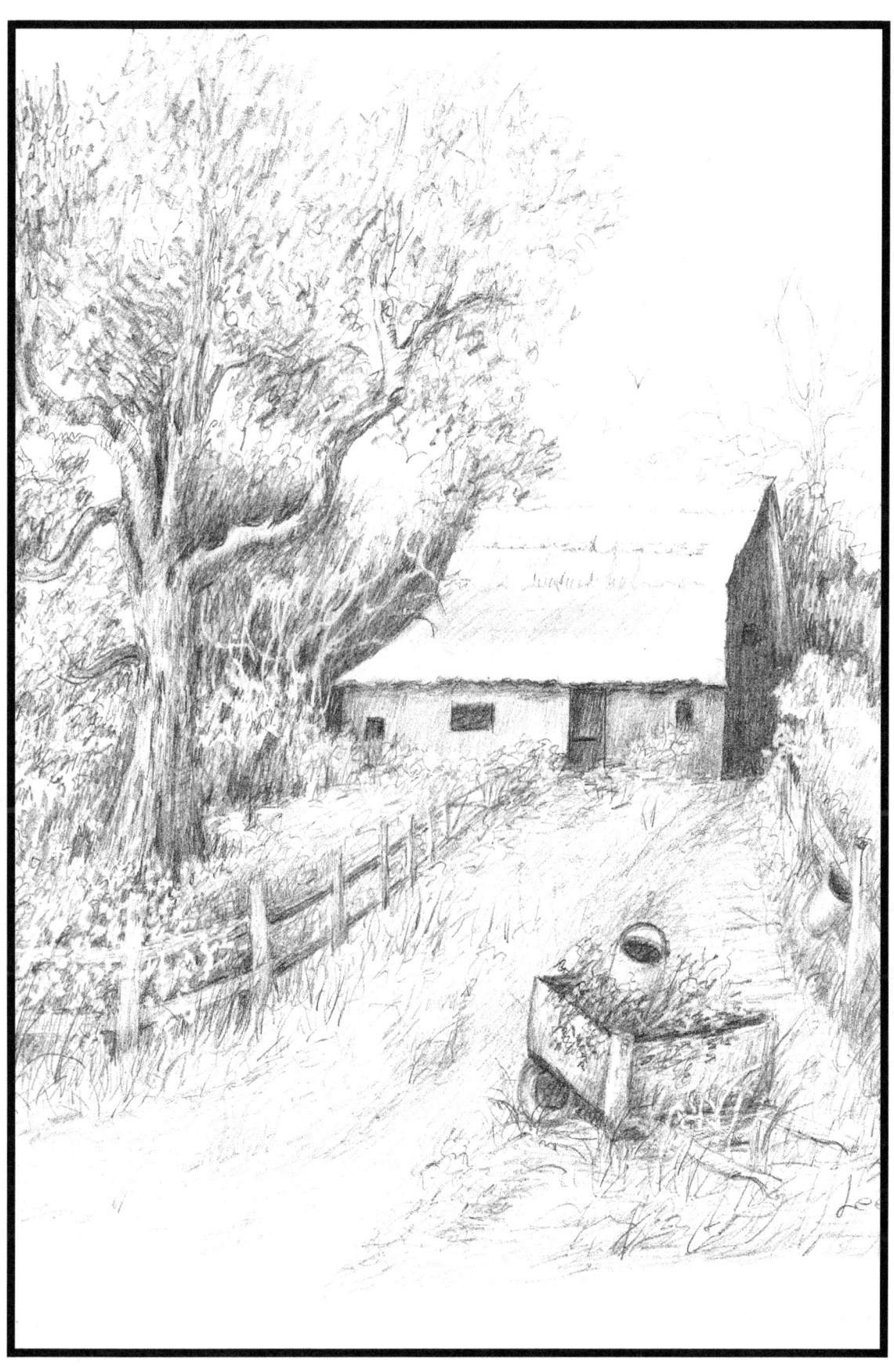

COLORING ART (COLORING BOOK FOR BIG KIDS) BOOK 1

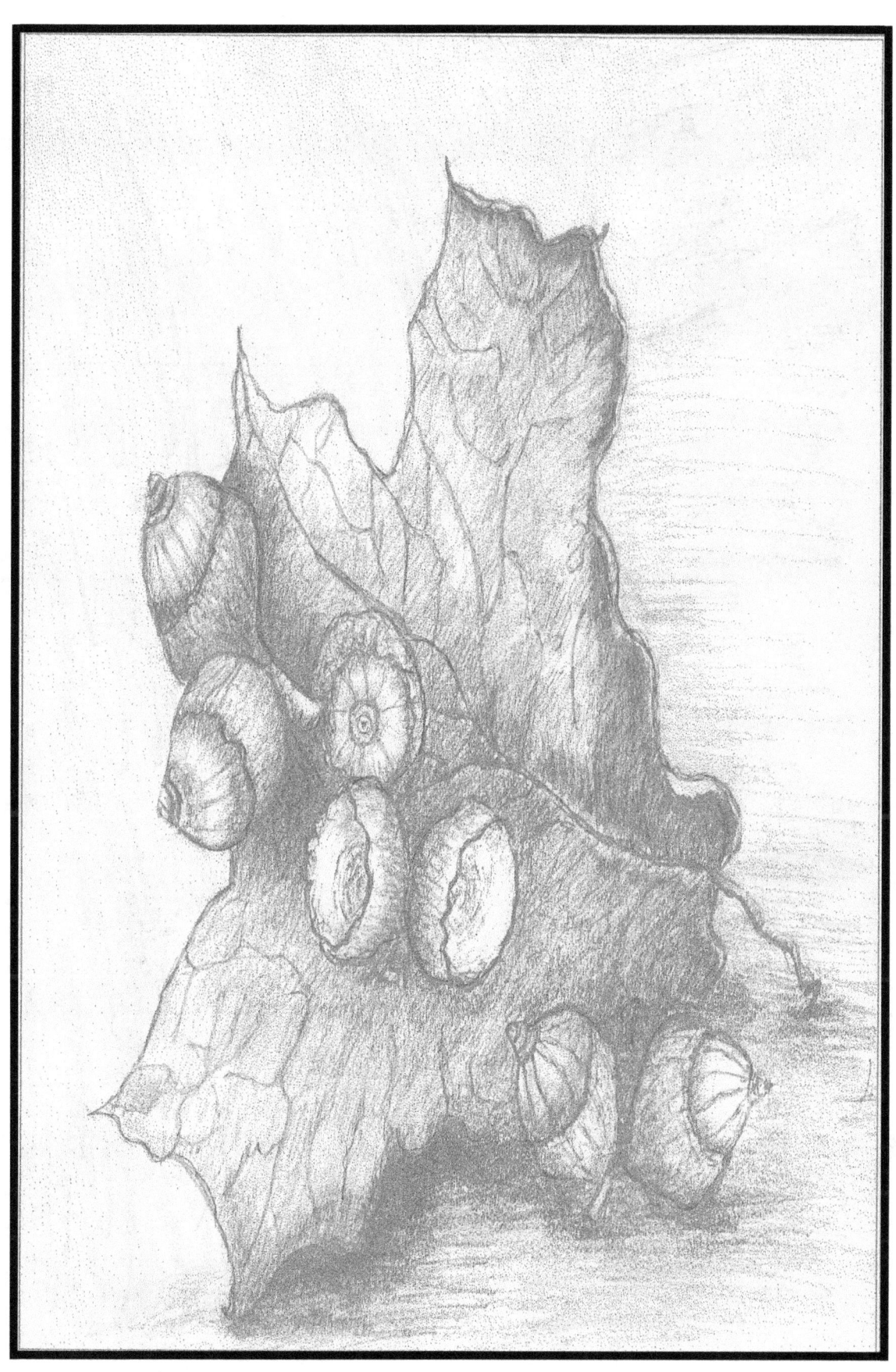

COLORING ART (COLORING BOOK FOR BIG KIDS) BOOK 1

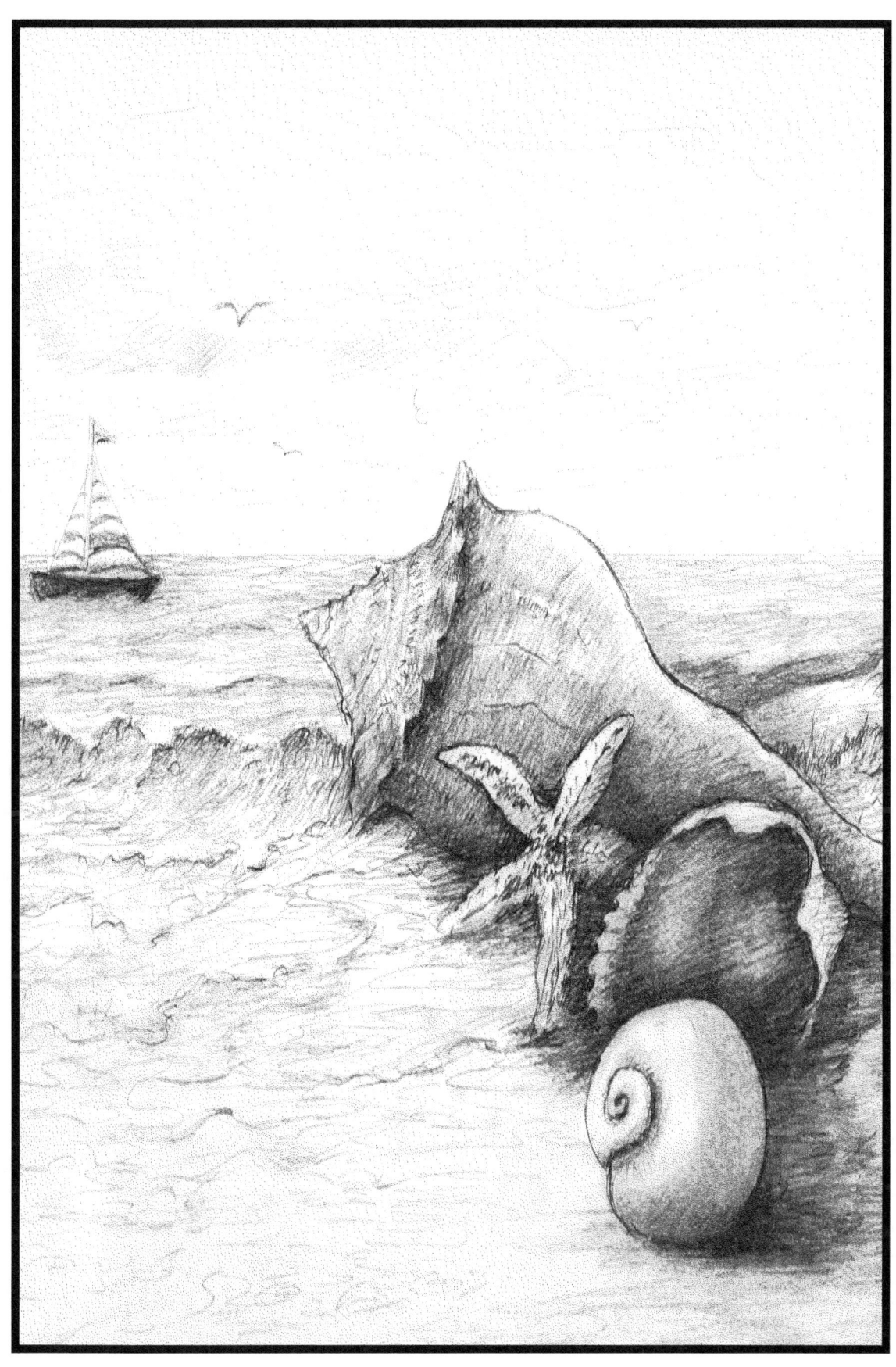

COLORING ART (COLORING BOOK FOR BIG KIDS) BOOK 1

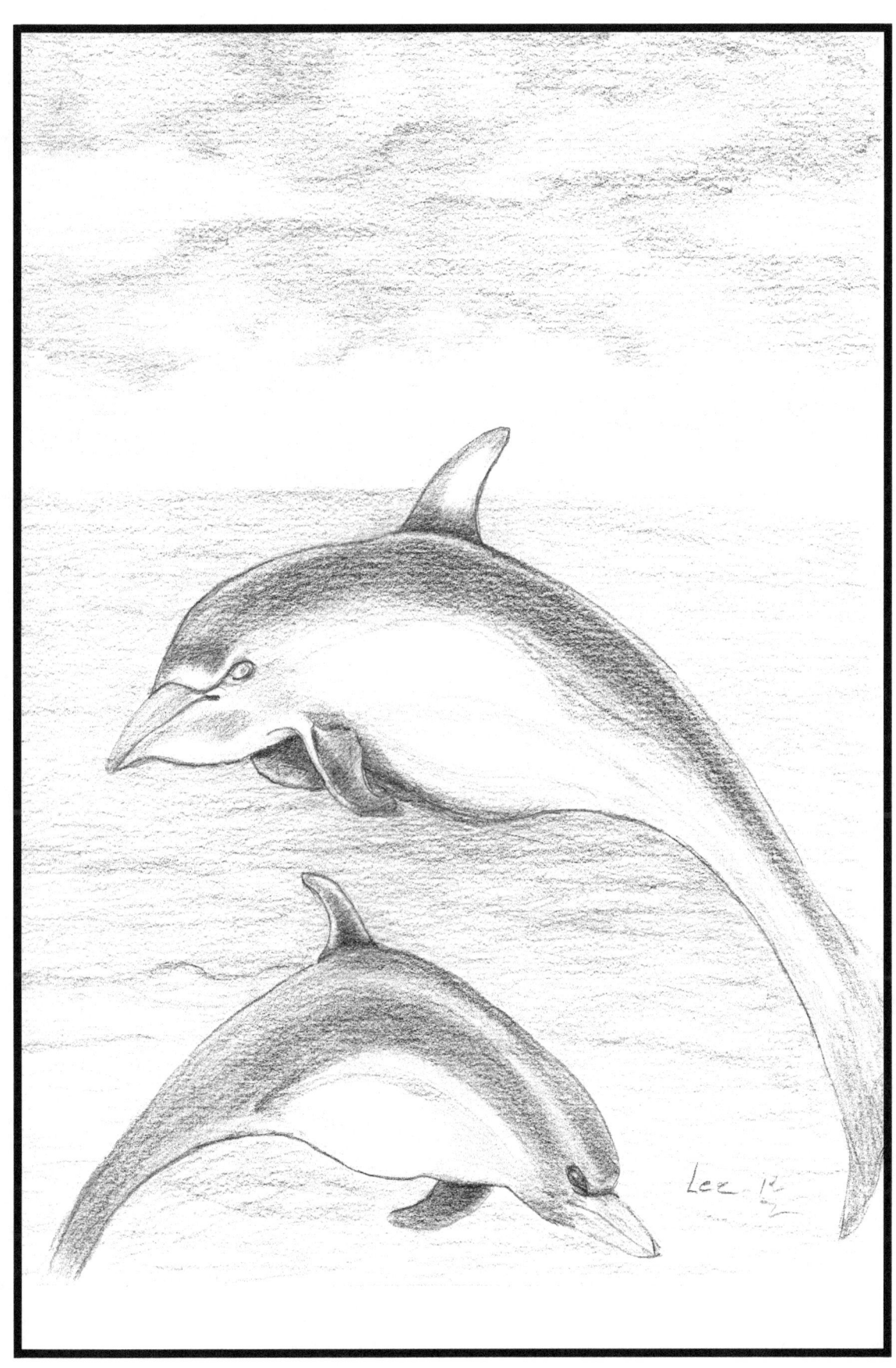

COLORING ART (COLORING BOOK FOR BIG KIDS) BOOK 1

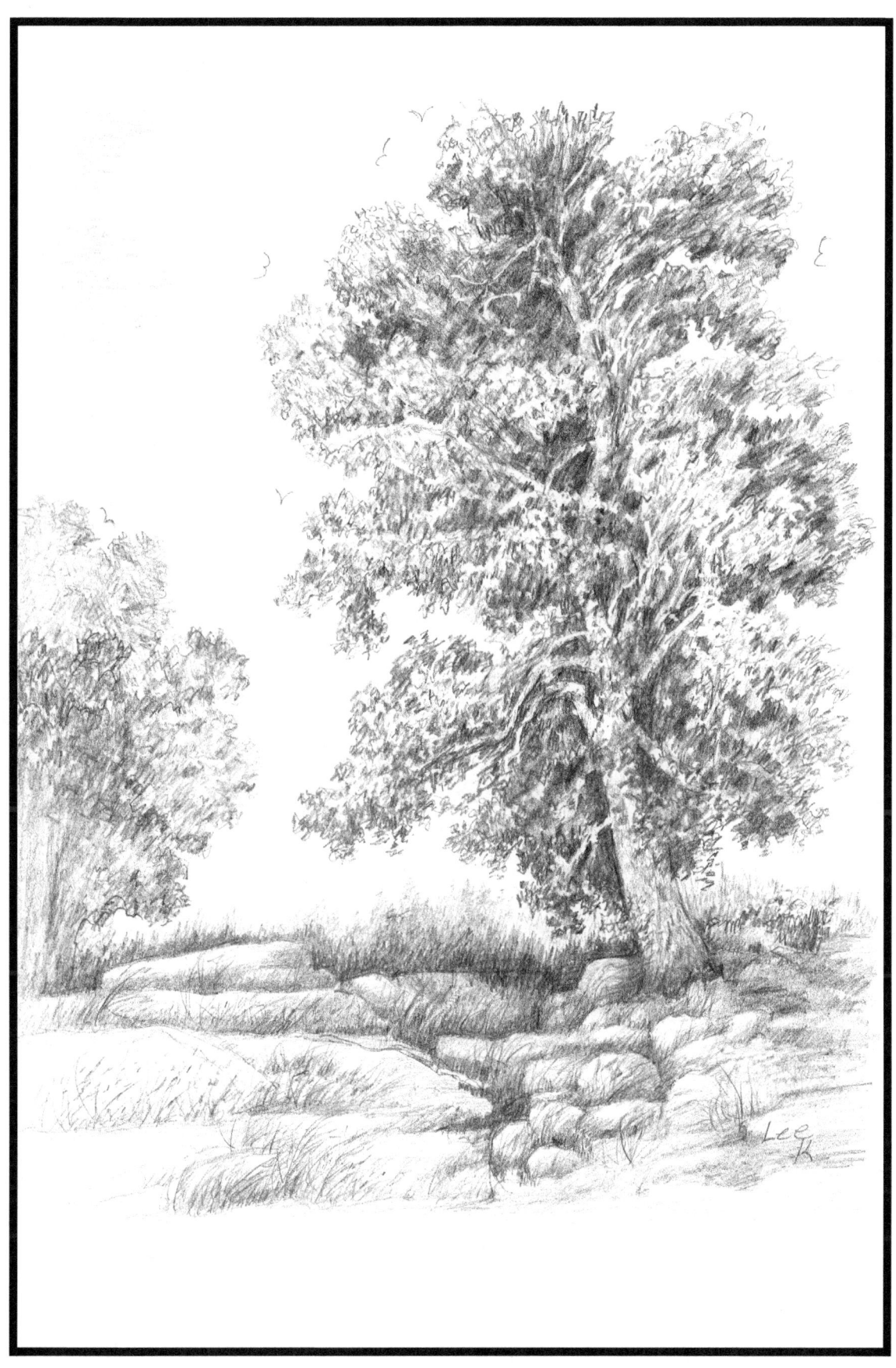

COLORING ART (COLORING BOOK FOR BIG KIDS) BOOK 1

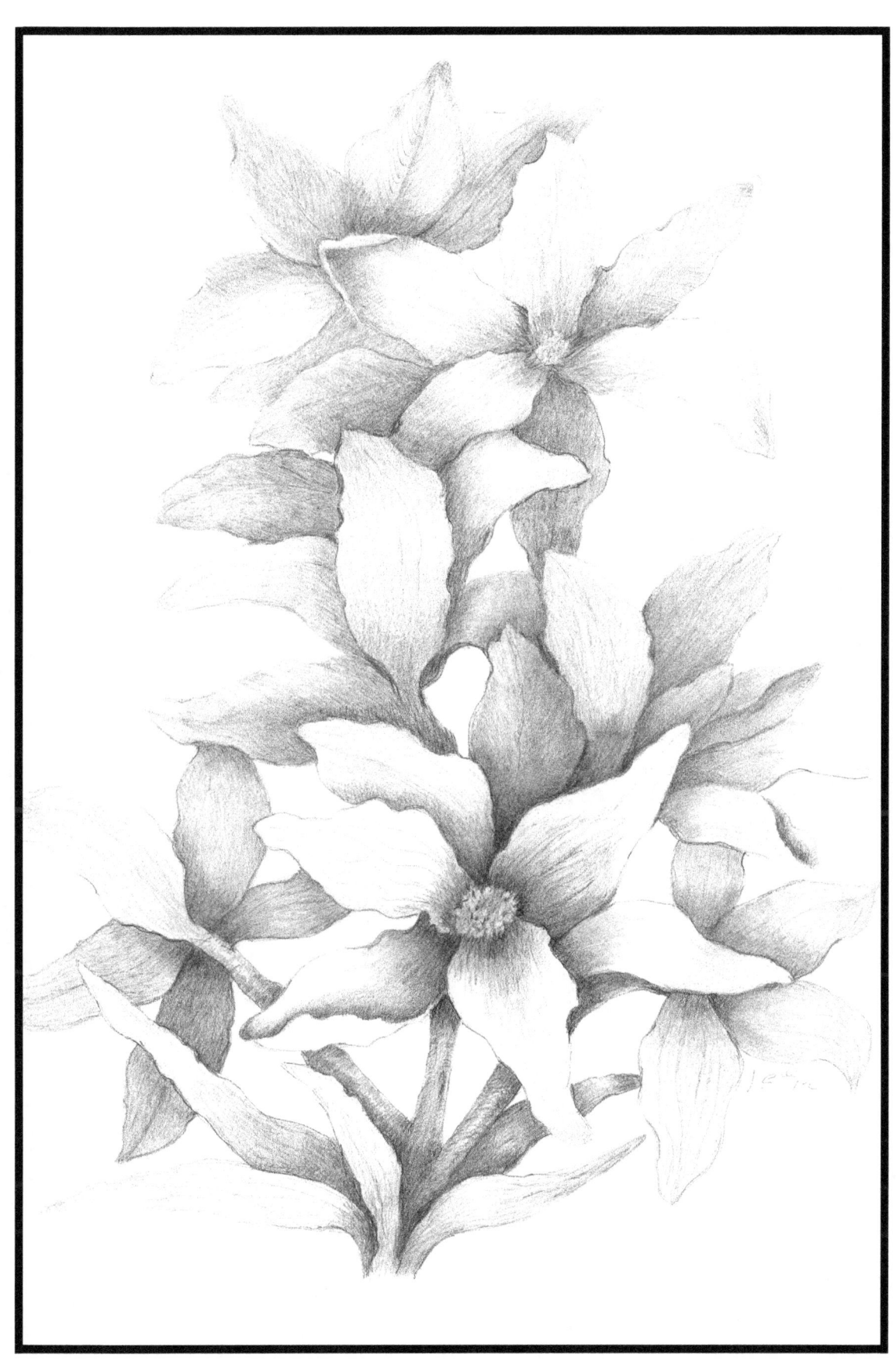

COLORING ART (COLORING BOOK FOR BIG KIDS) BOOK 1

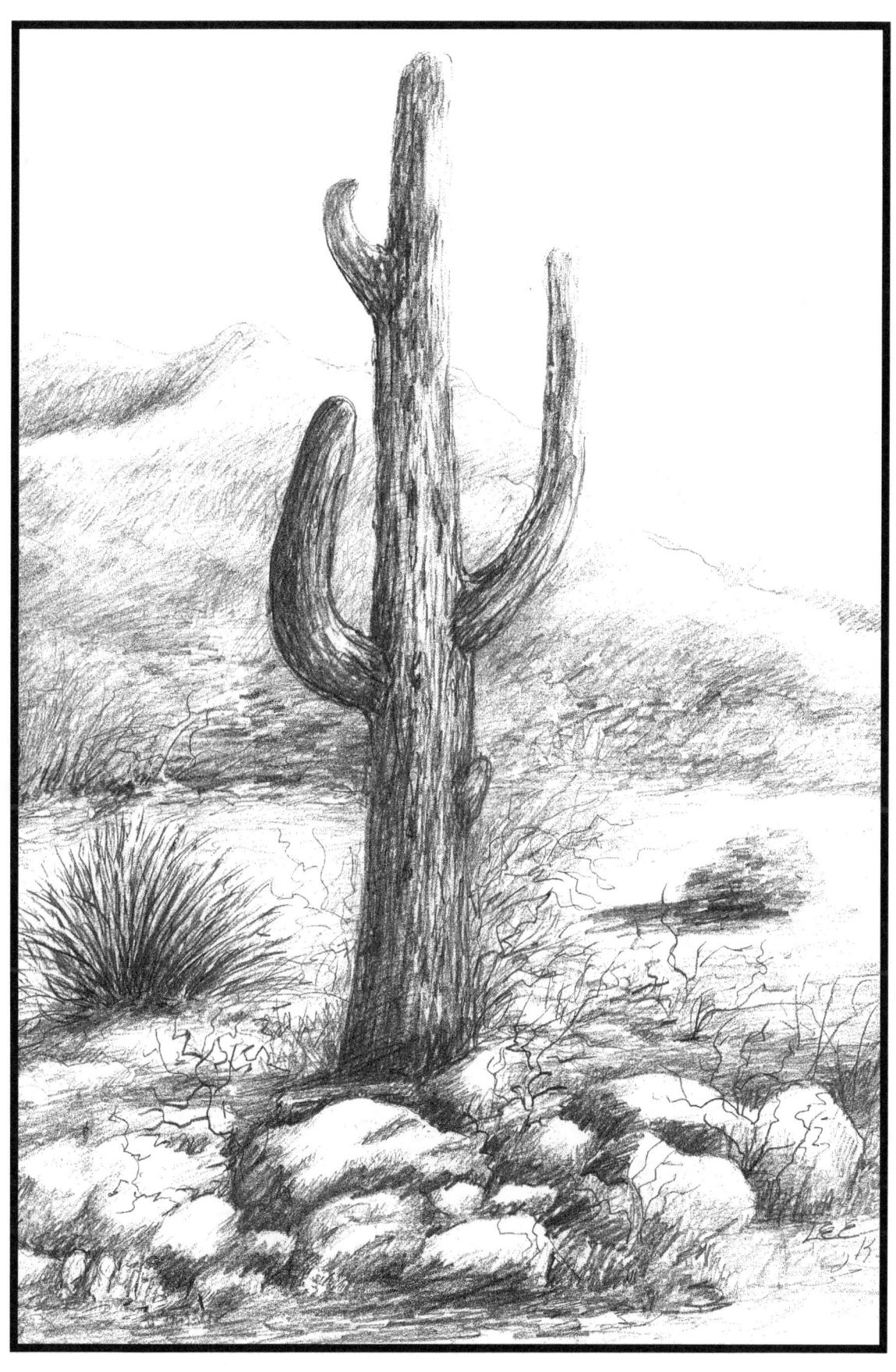

COLORING ART (COLORING BOOK FOR BIG KIDS) BOOK 1

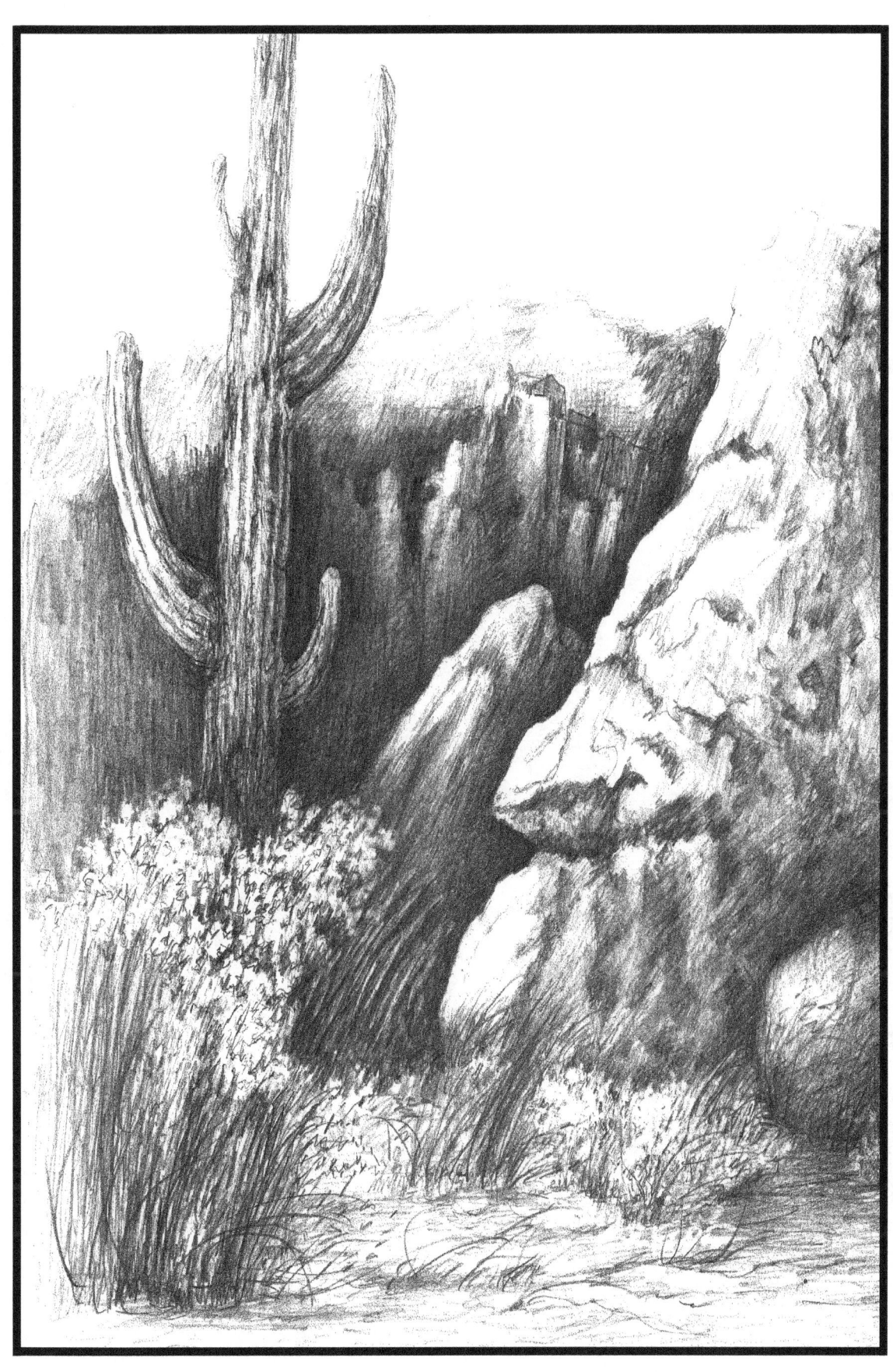

COLORING ART (COLORING BOOK FOR BIG KIDS) BOOK 1

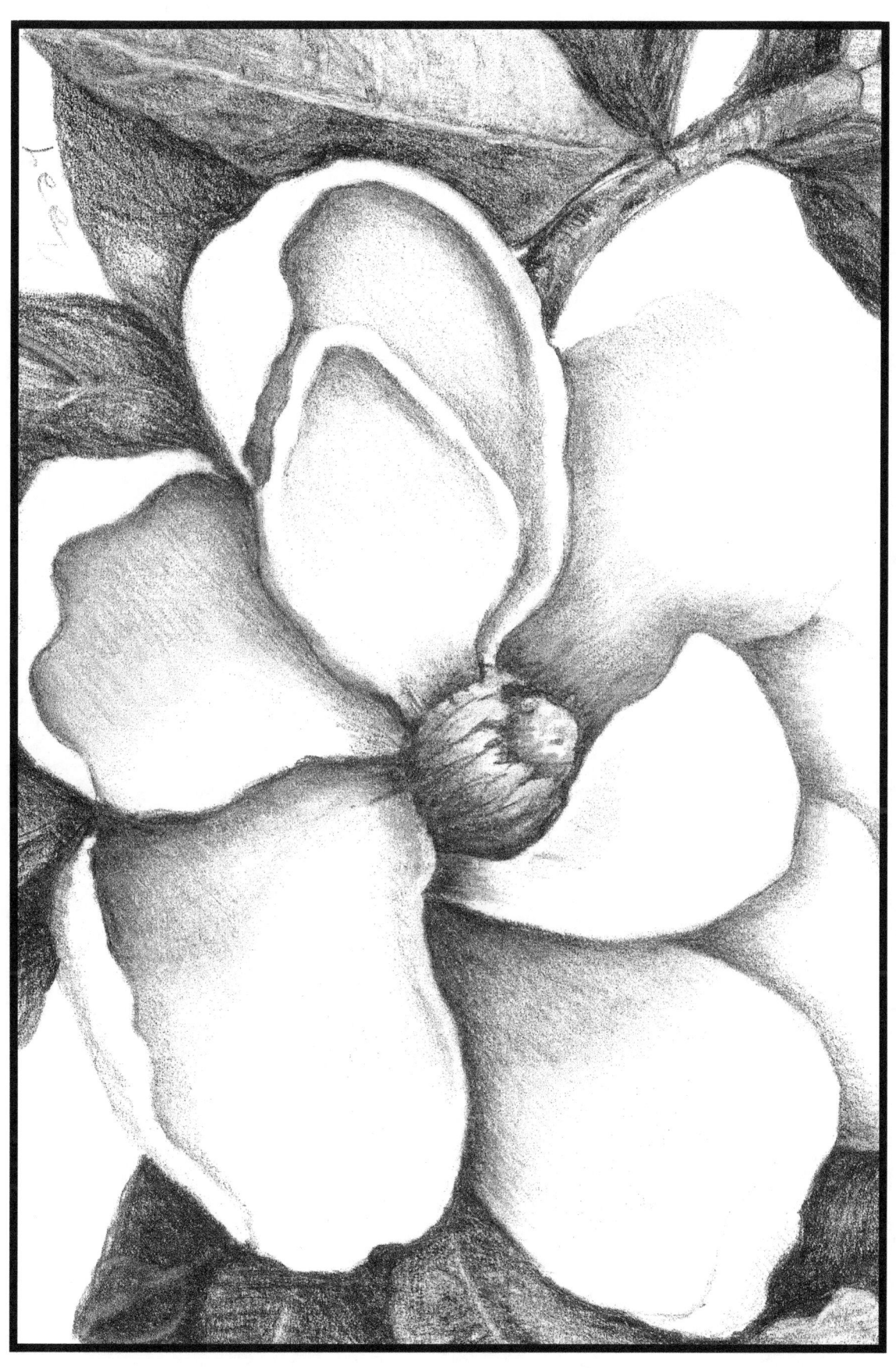

COLORING ART (COLORING BOOK FOR BIG KIDS) BOOK 1

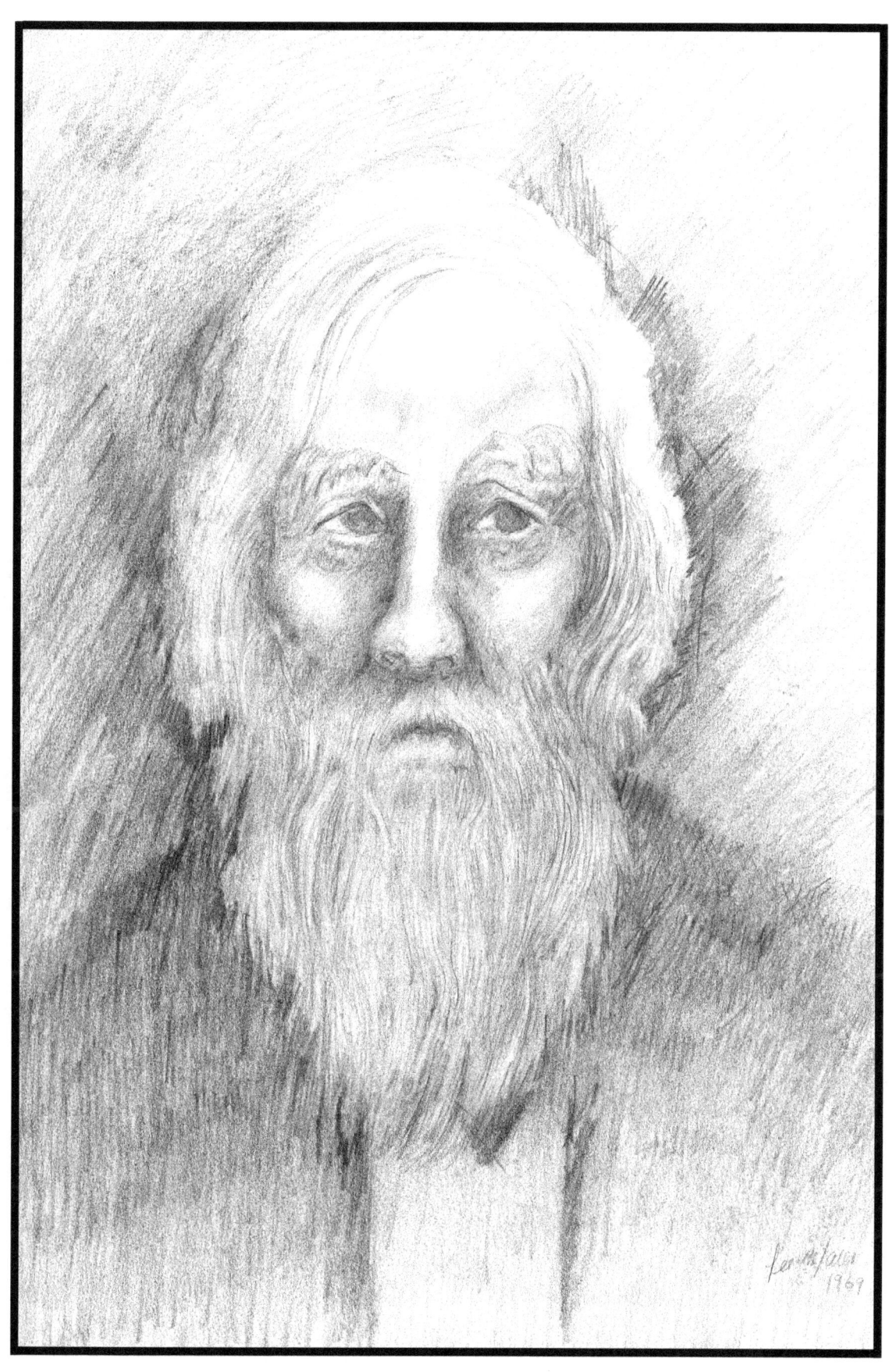

COLORING ART (COLORING BOOK FOR BIG KIDS) BOOK 1

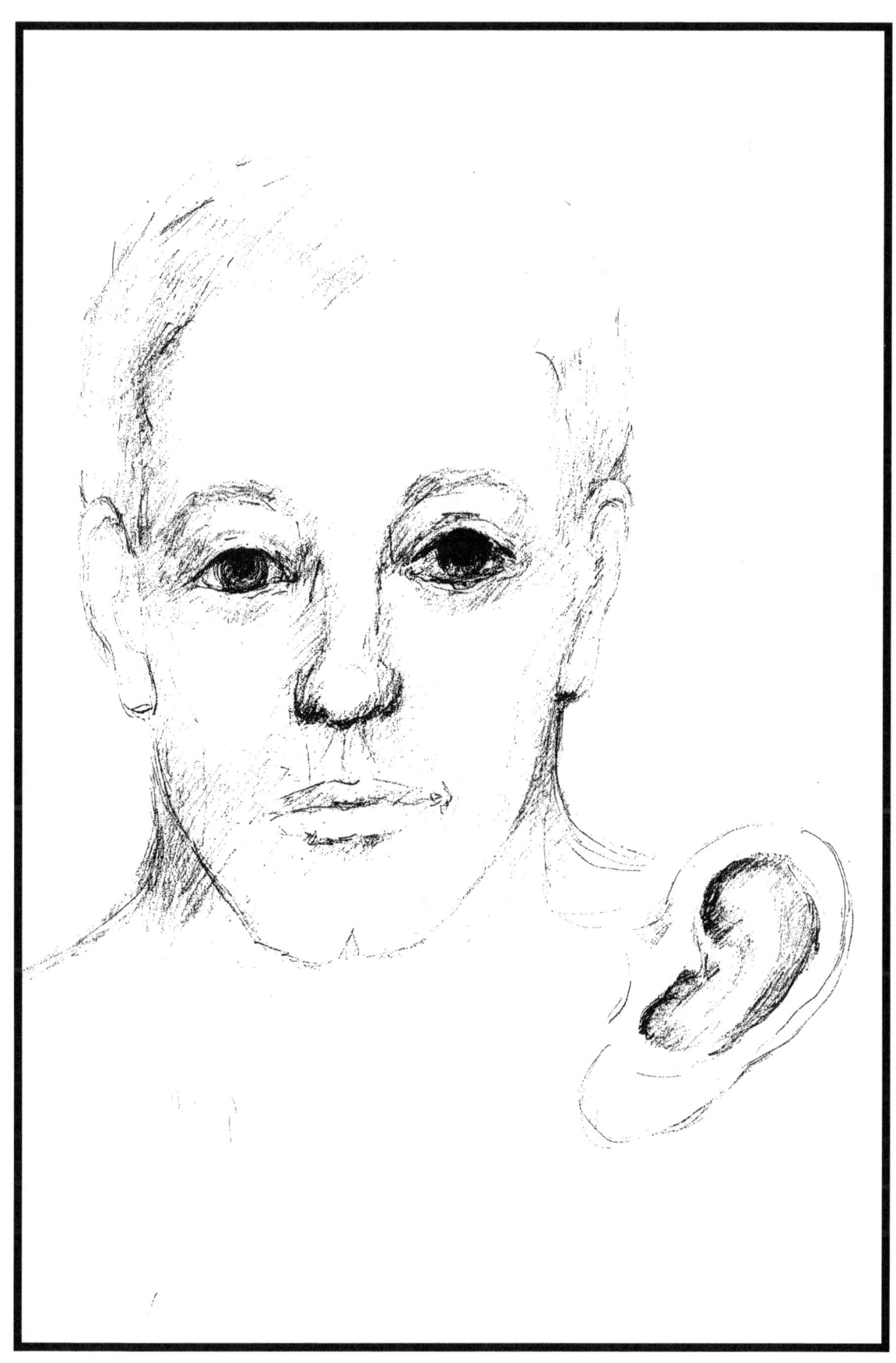

COLORING ART (COLORING BOOK FOR BIG KIDS) BOOK 1

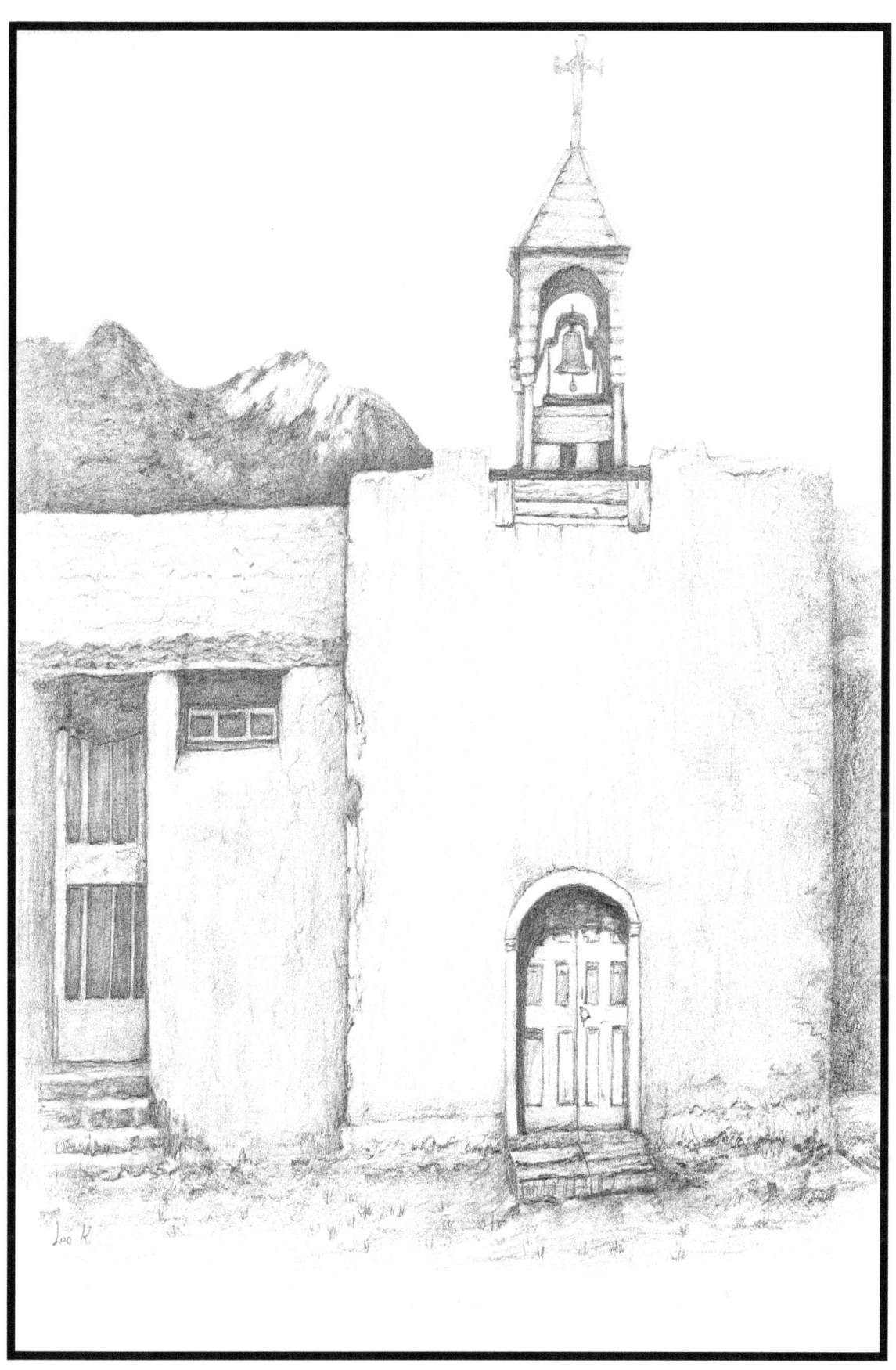

COLORING ART (COLORING BOOK FOR BIG KIDS) BOOK 1

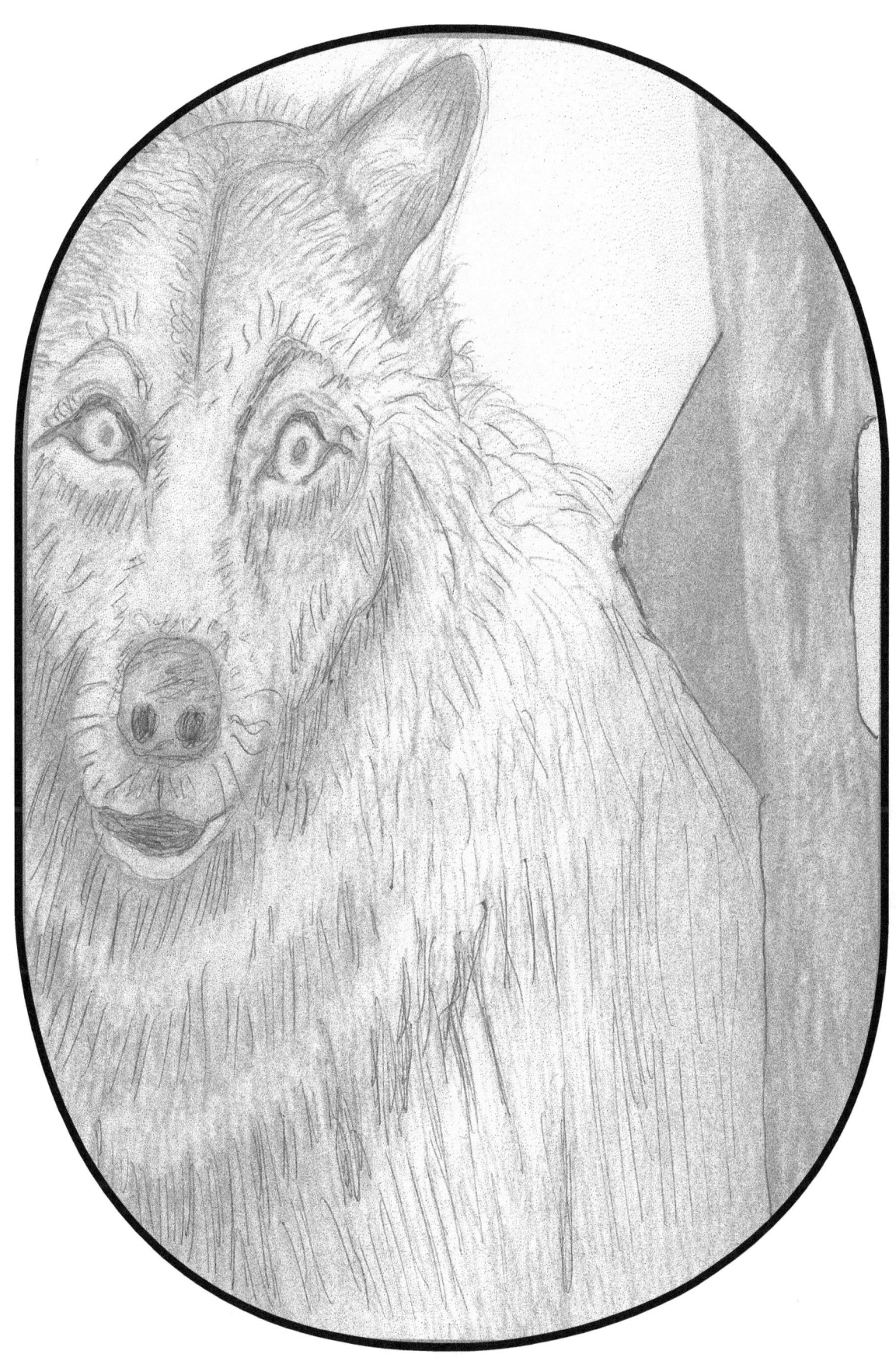

COLORING ART (COLORING BOOK FOR BIG KIDS) BOOK 1

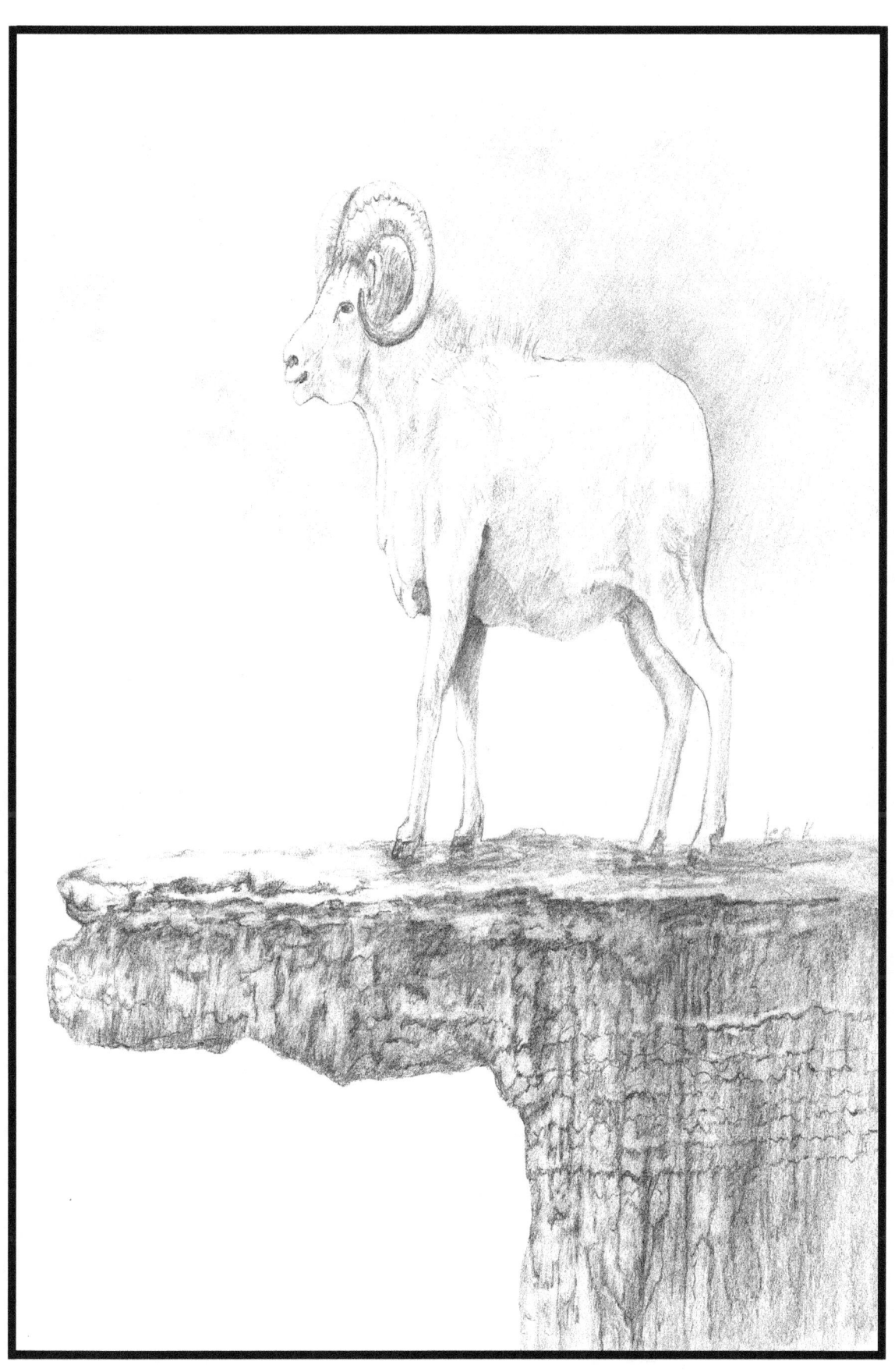

COLORING ART (COLORING BOOK FOR BIG KIDS) BOOK 1

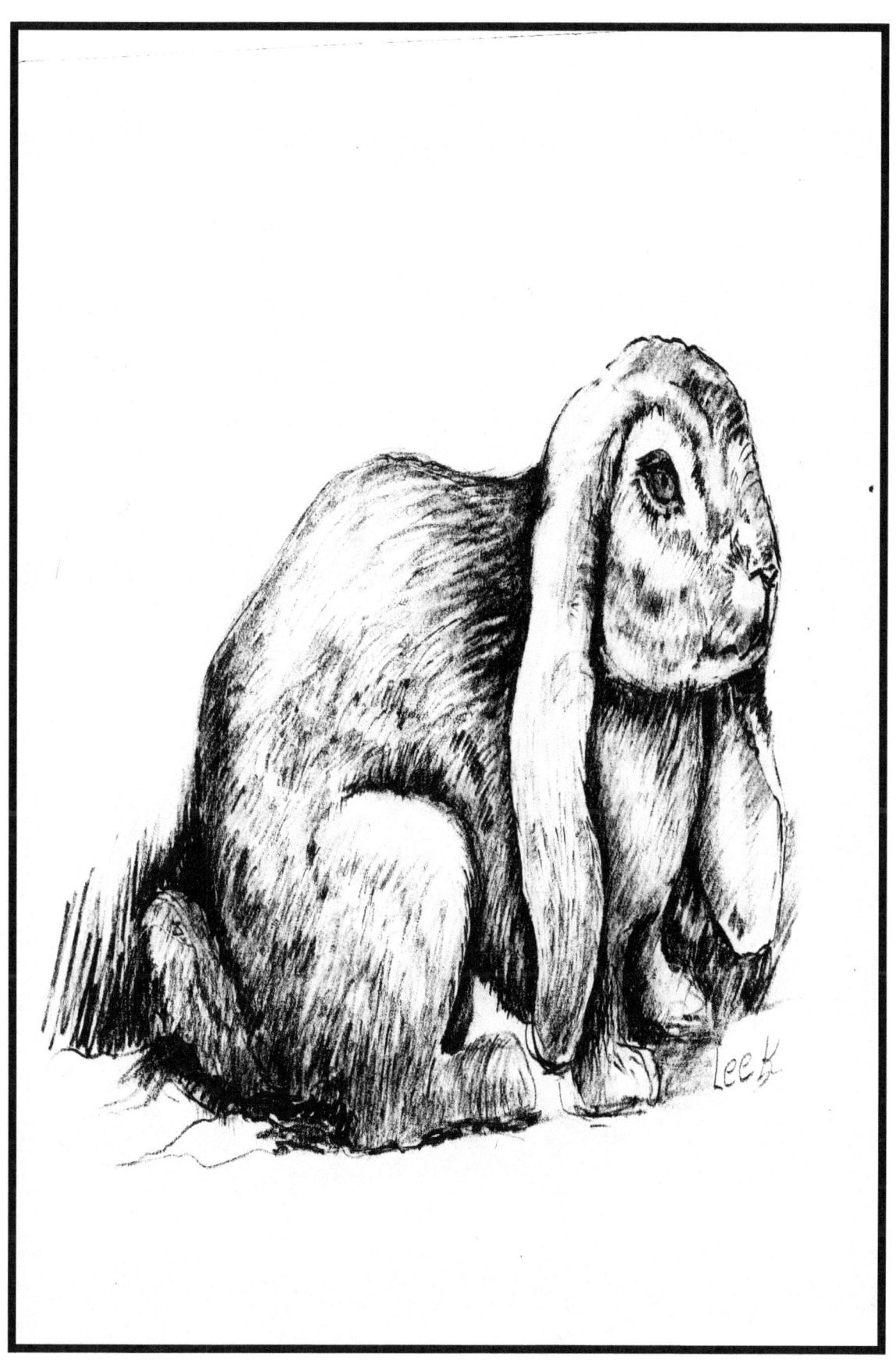

COLORING ART (COLORING BOOK FOR BIG KIDS) BOOK 1

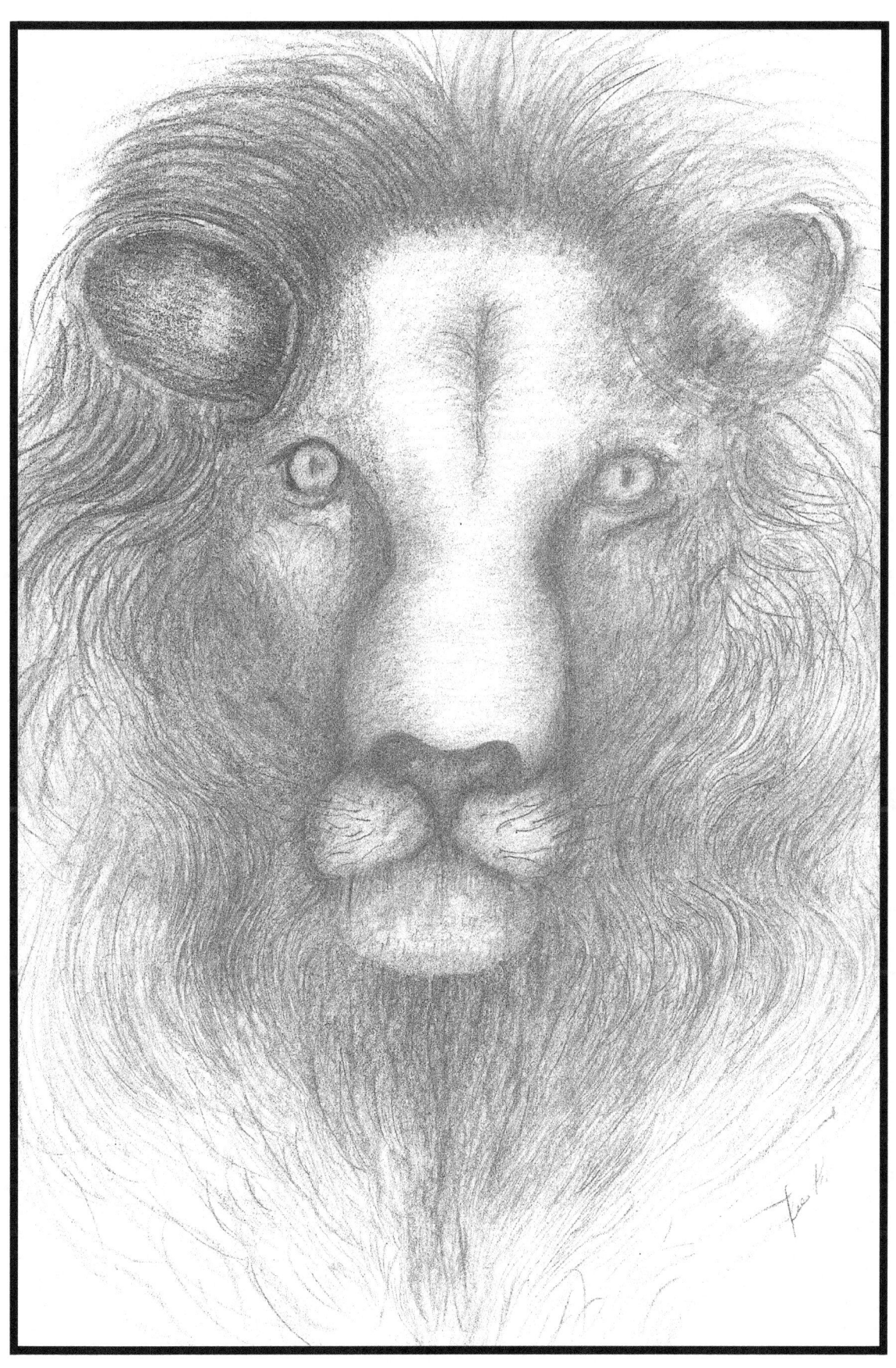

COLORING ART (COLORING BOOK FOR BIG KIDS) BOOK 1

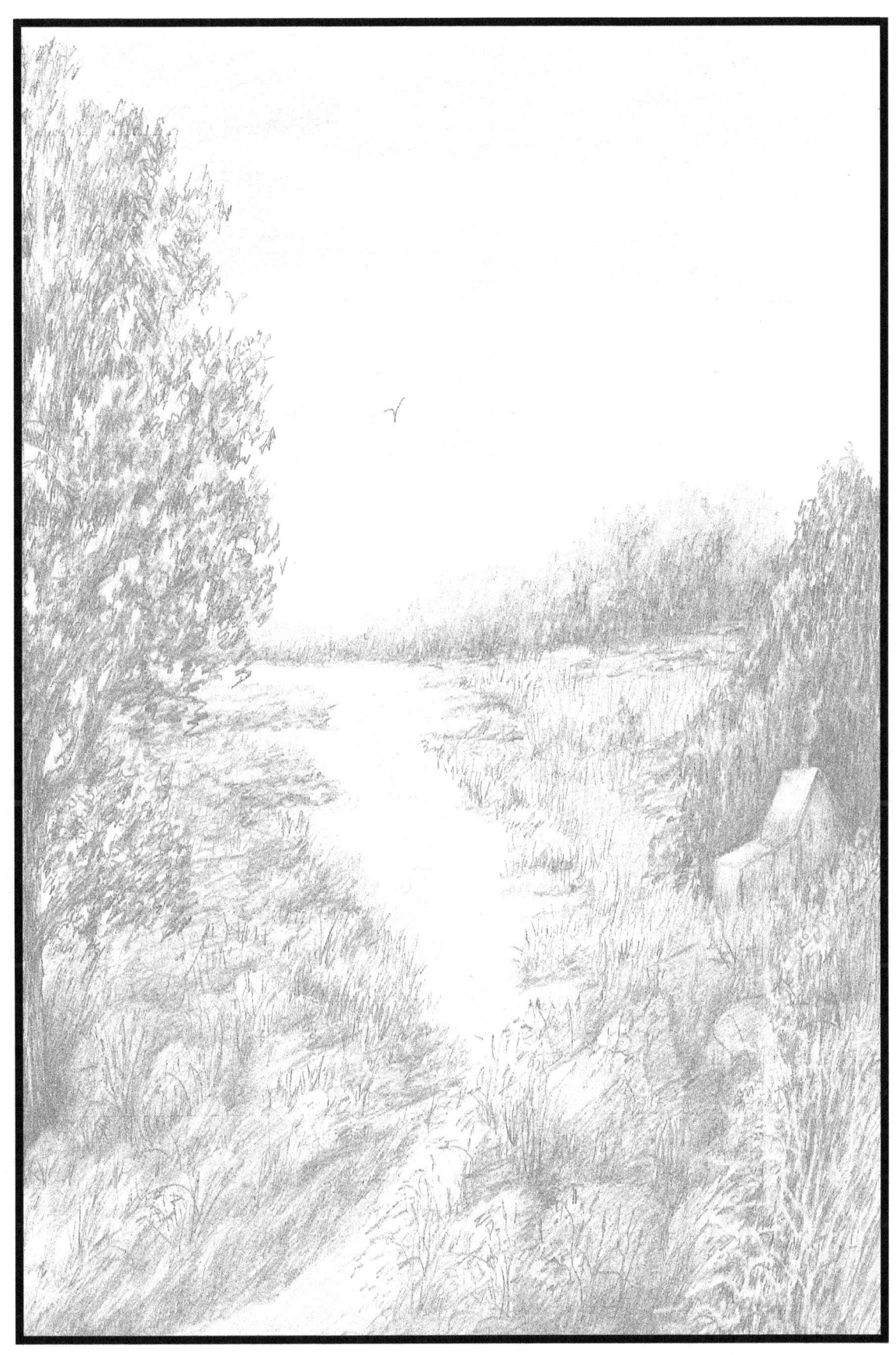

COLORING ART (COLORING BOOK FOR BIG KIDS) BOOK 1

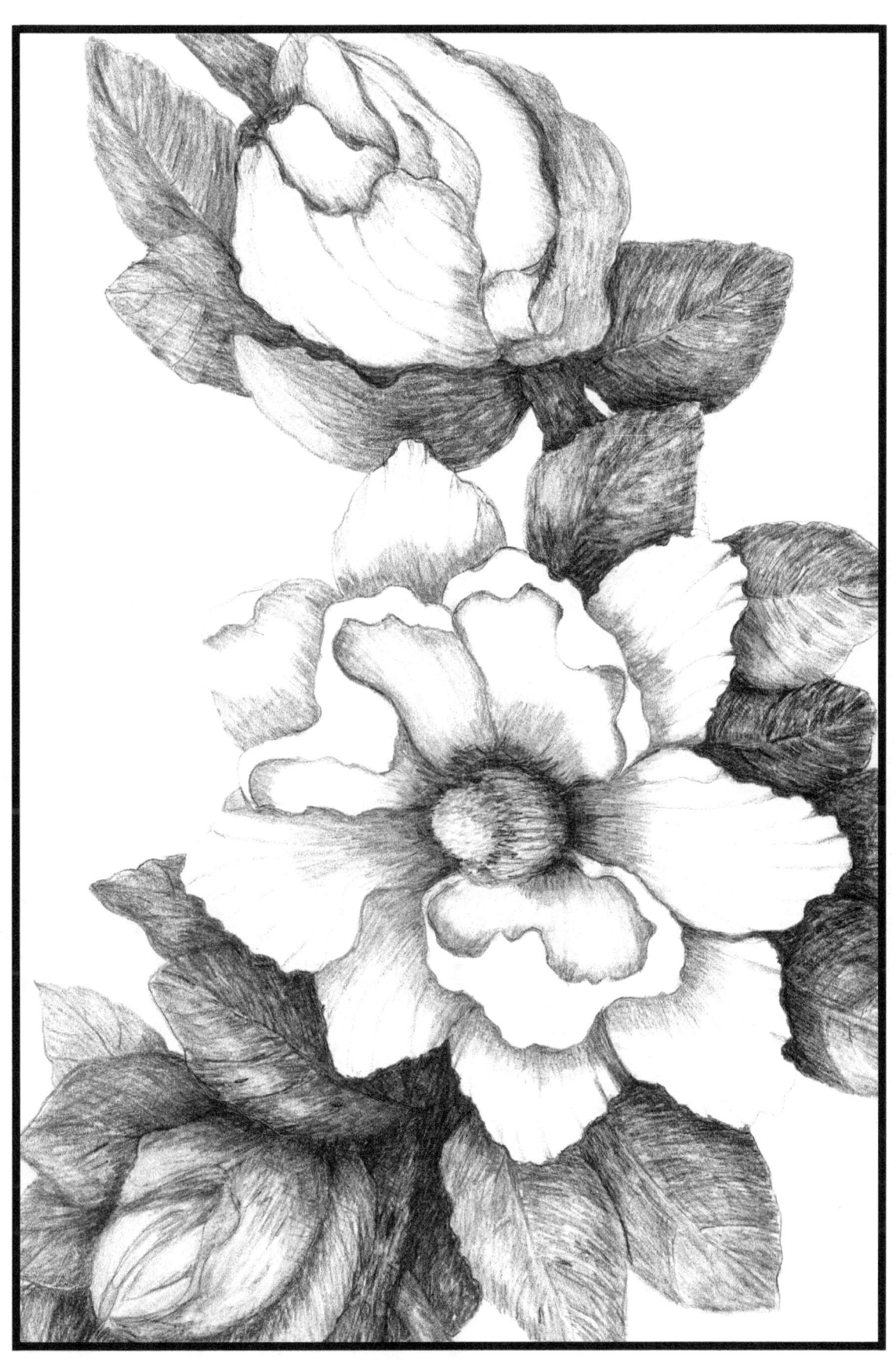

COLORING ART (COLORING BOOK FOR BIG KIDS) BOOK 1

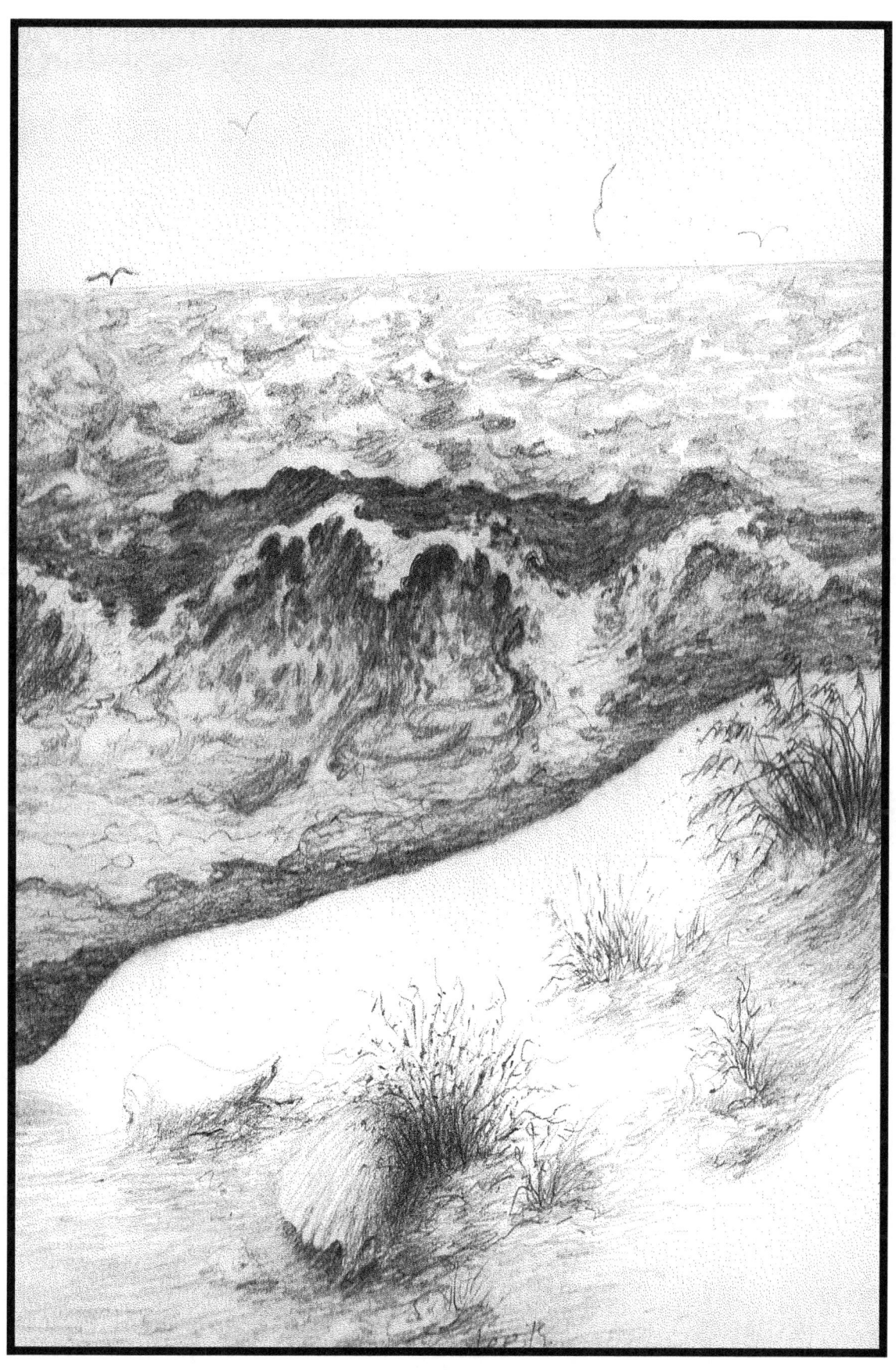

COLORING ART (COLORING BOOK FOR BIG KIDS) BOOK 1

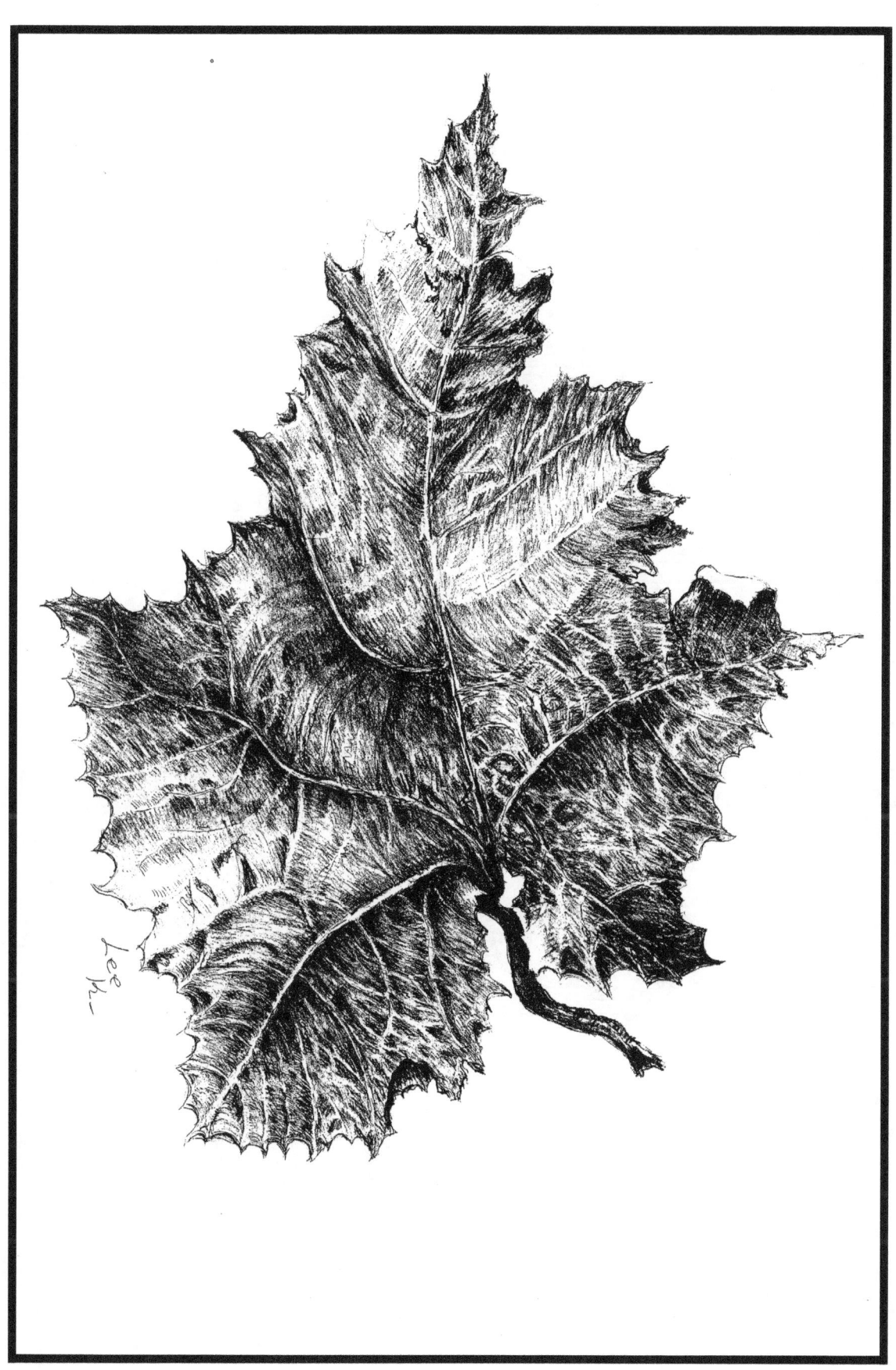

COLORING ART (COLORING BOOK FOR BIG KIDS) BOOK 1

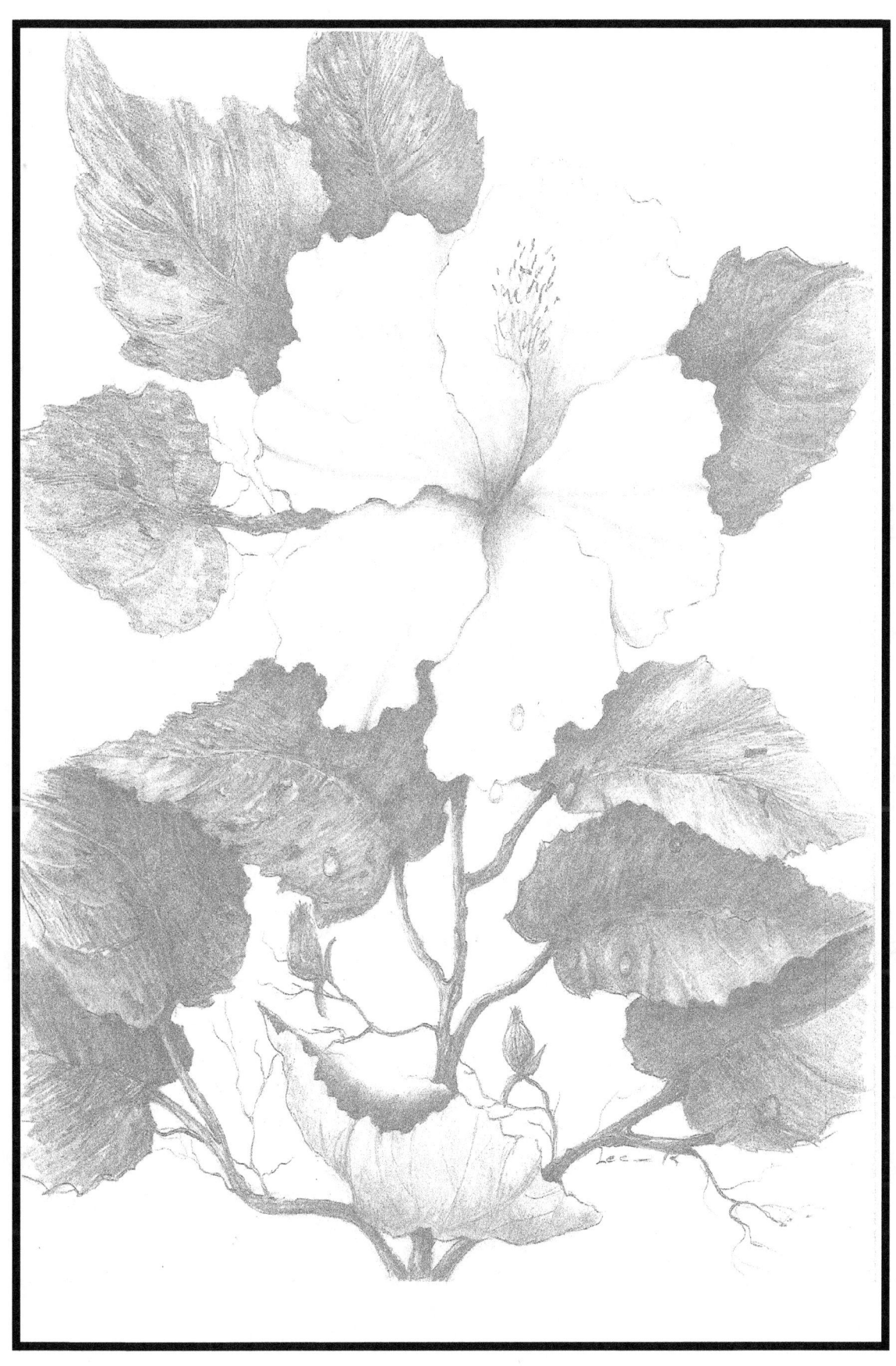

COLORING ART (COLORING BOOK FOR BIG KIDS) BOOK 1

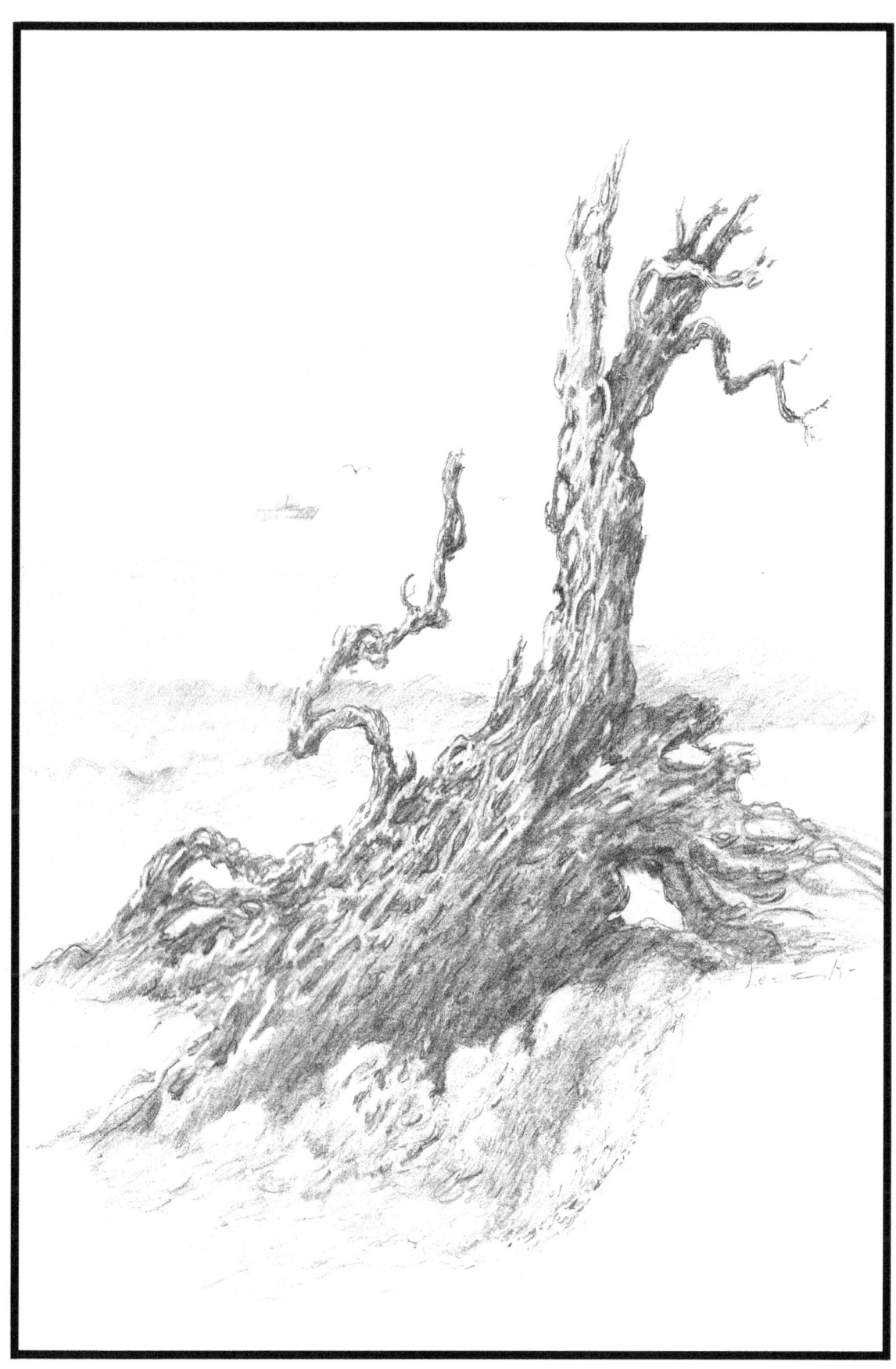

COLORING ART (COLORING BOOK FOR BIG KIDS) BOOK 1

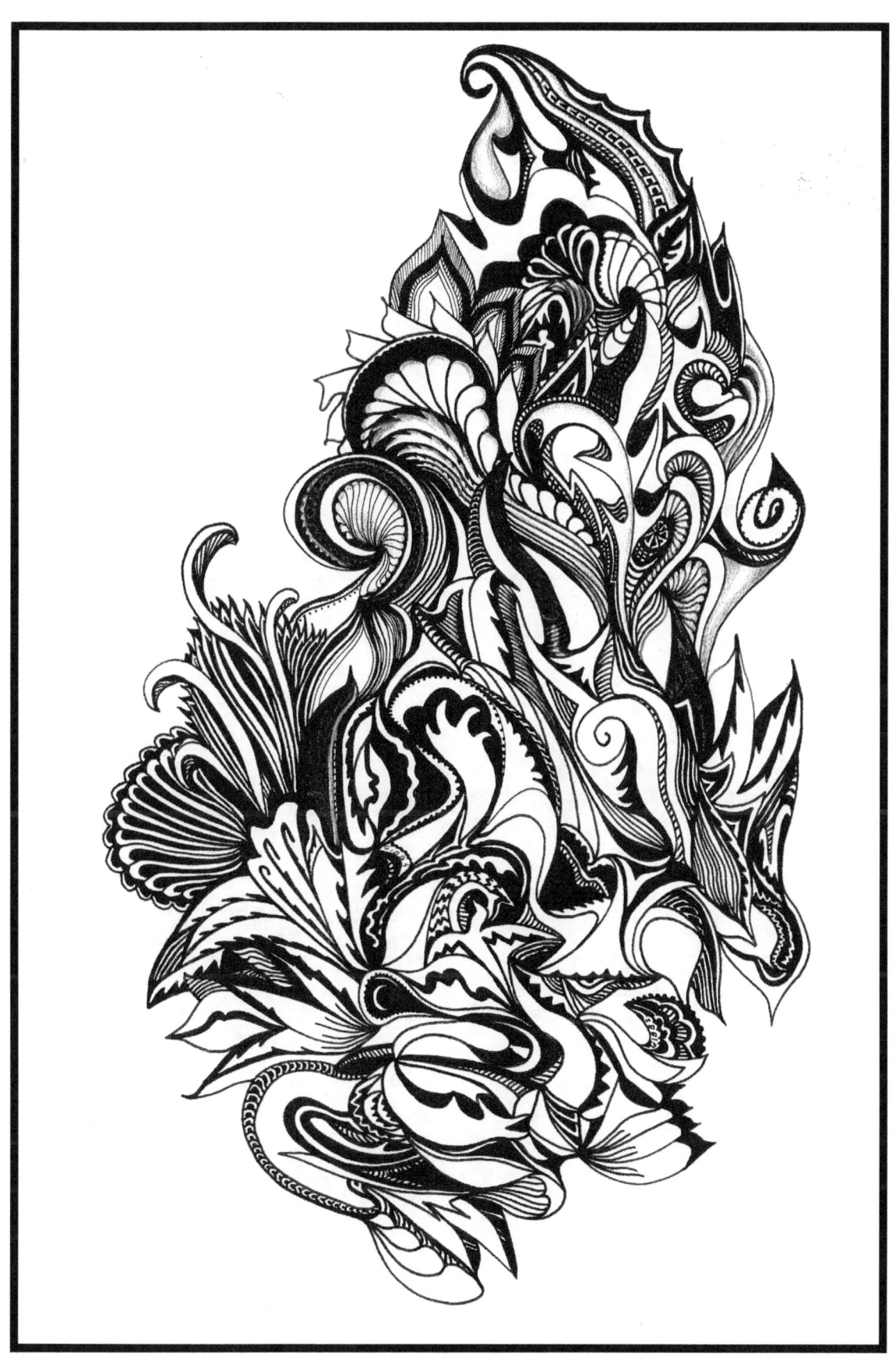

COLORING ART (COLORING BOOK FOR BIG KIDS) BOOK 1

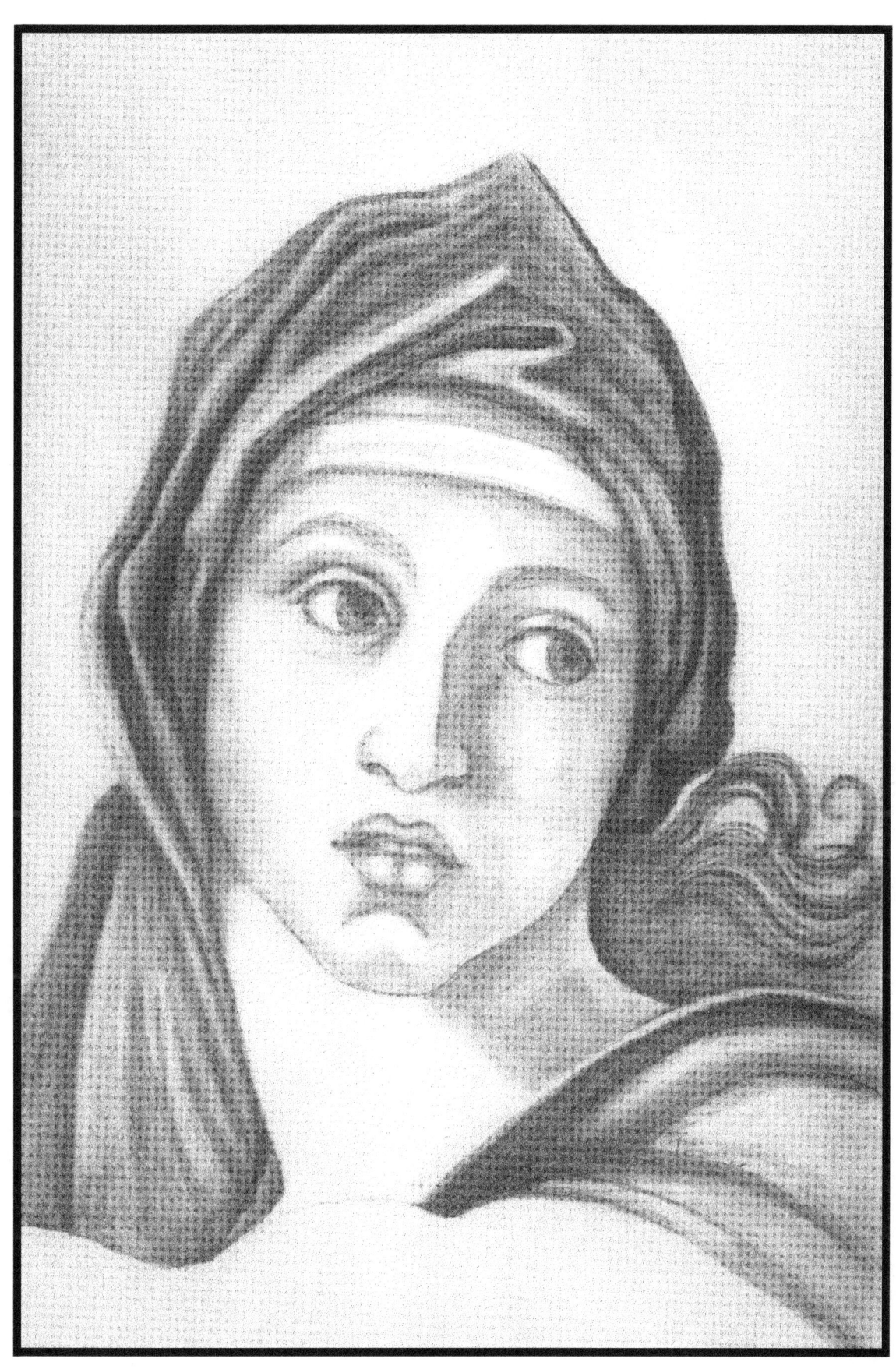

COLORING ART (COLORING BOOK FOR BIG KIDS) BOOK 1

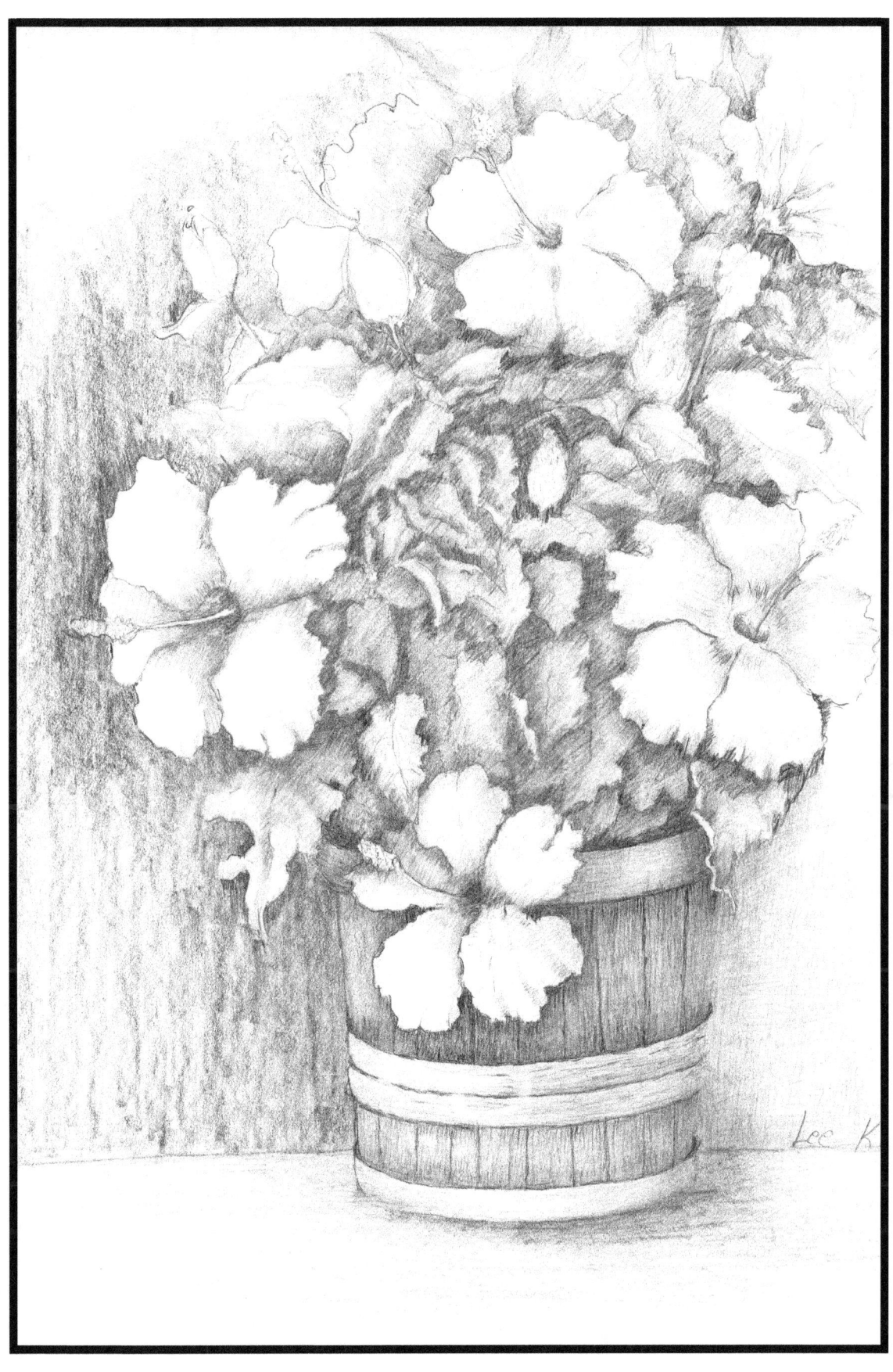

COLORING ART (COLORING BOOK FOR BIG KIDS) BOOK 1

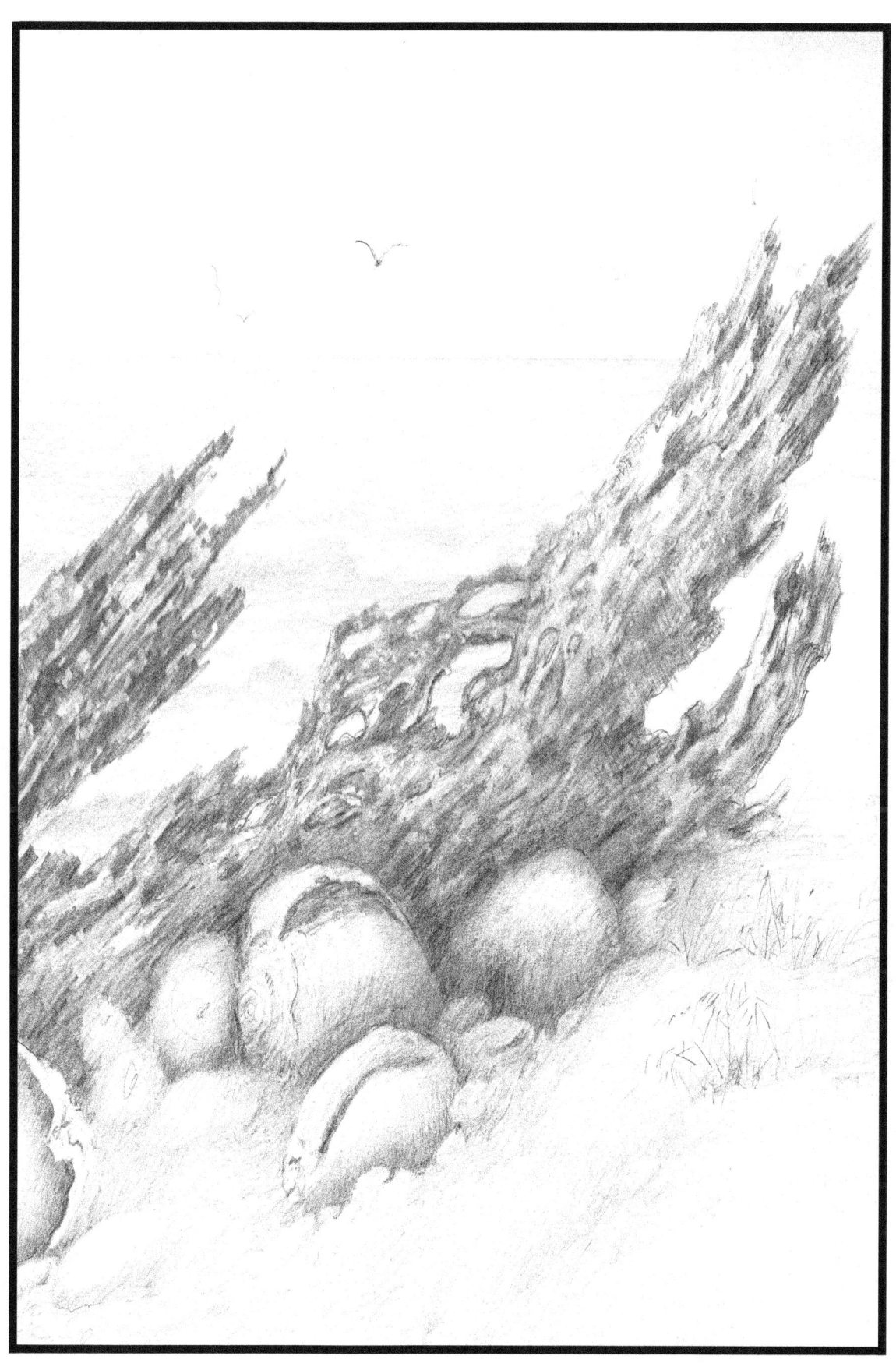

COLORING ART (COLORING BOOK FOR BIG KIDS) BOOK 1

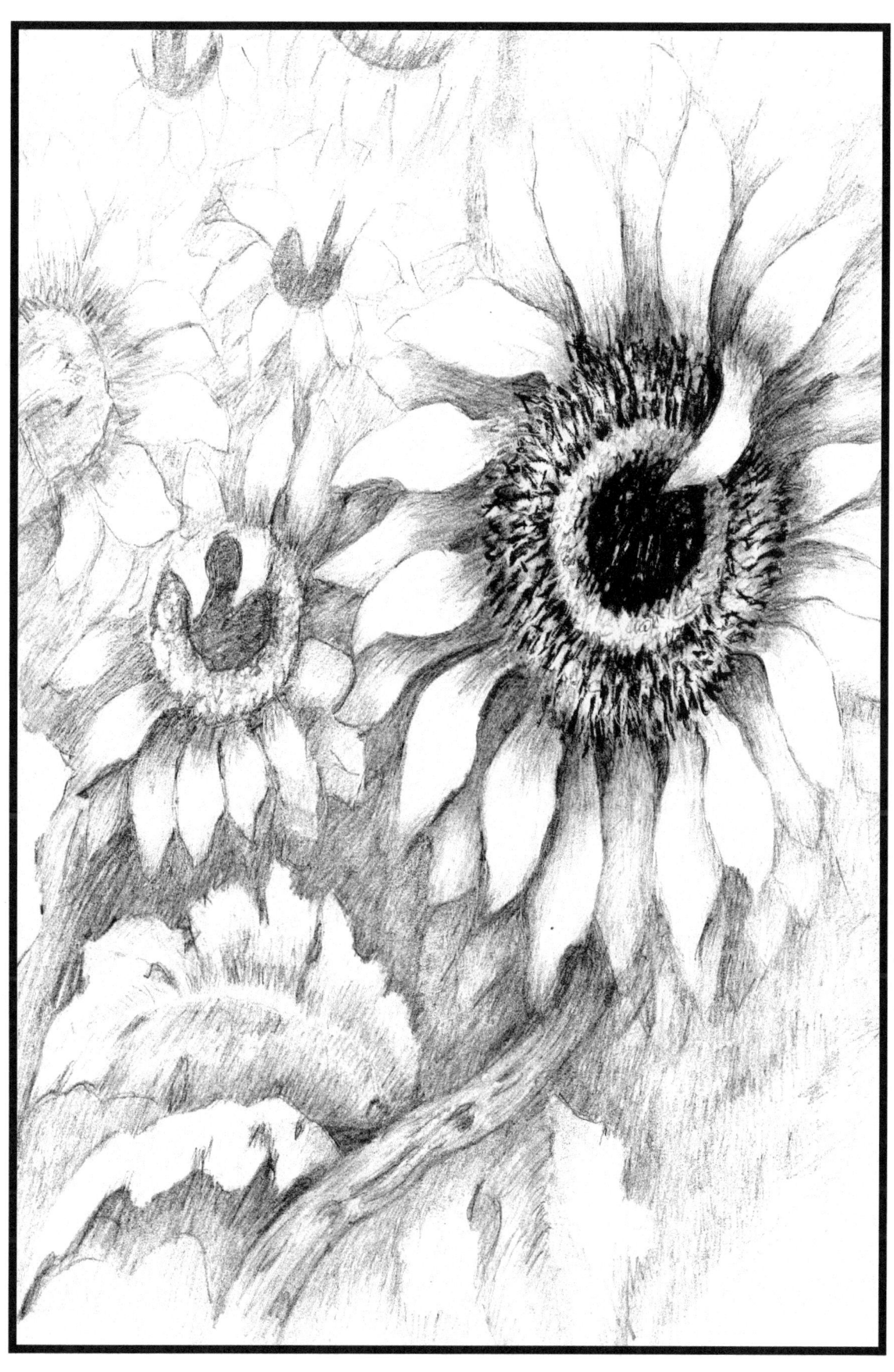

COLORING ART (COLORING BOOK FOR BIG KIDS) BOOK 1

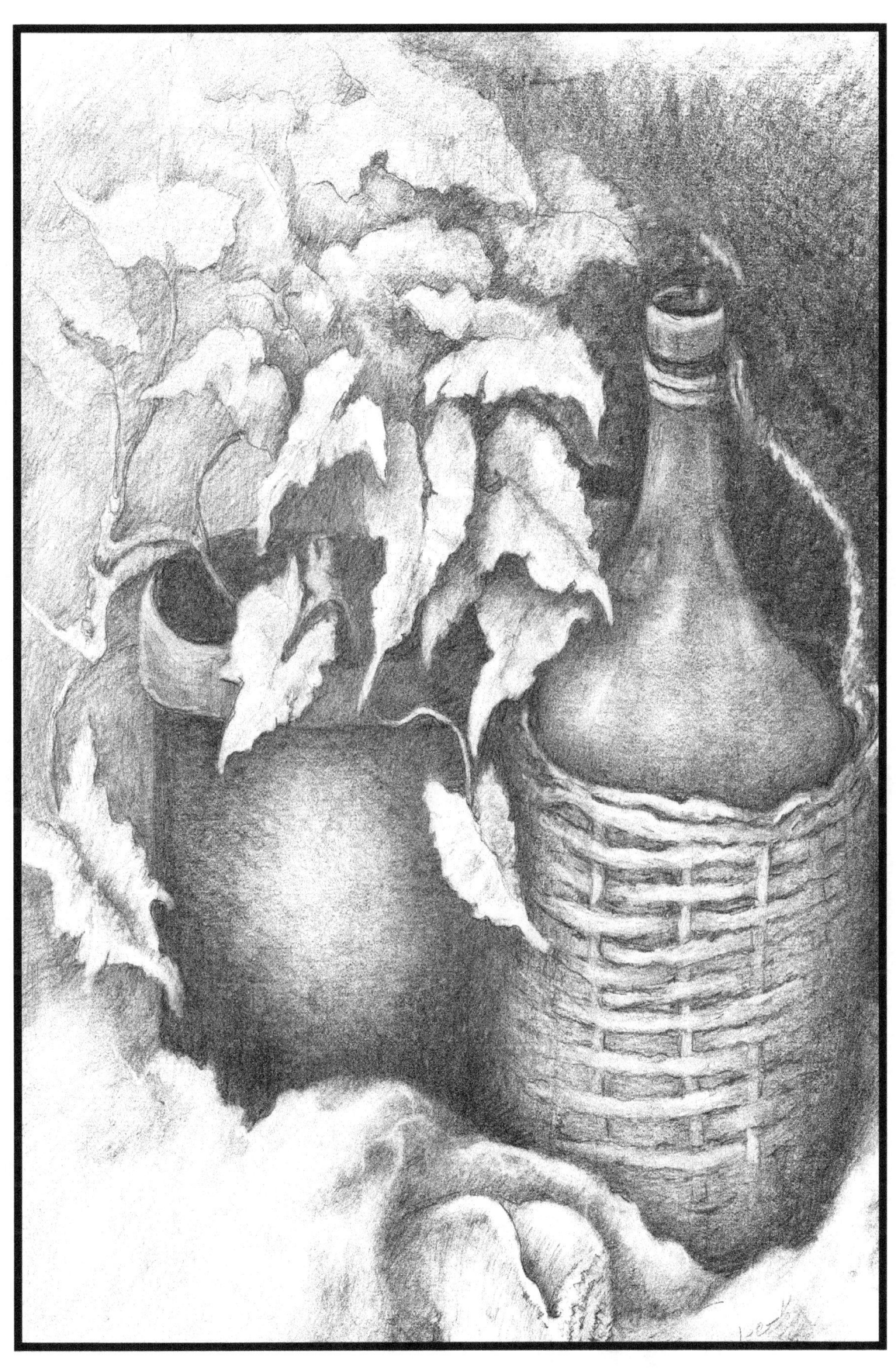

COLORING ART (COLORING BOOK FOR BIG KIDS) BOOK 1

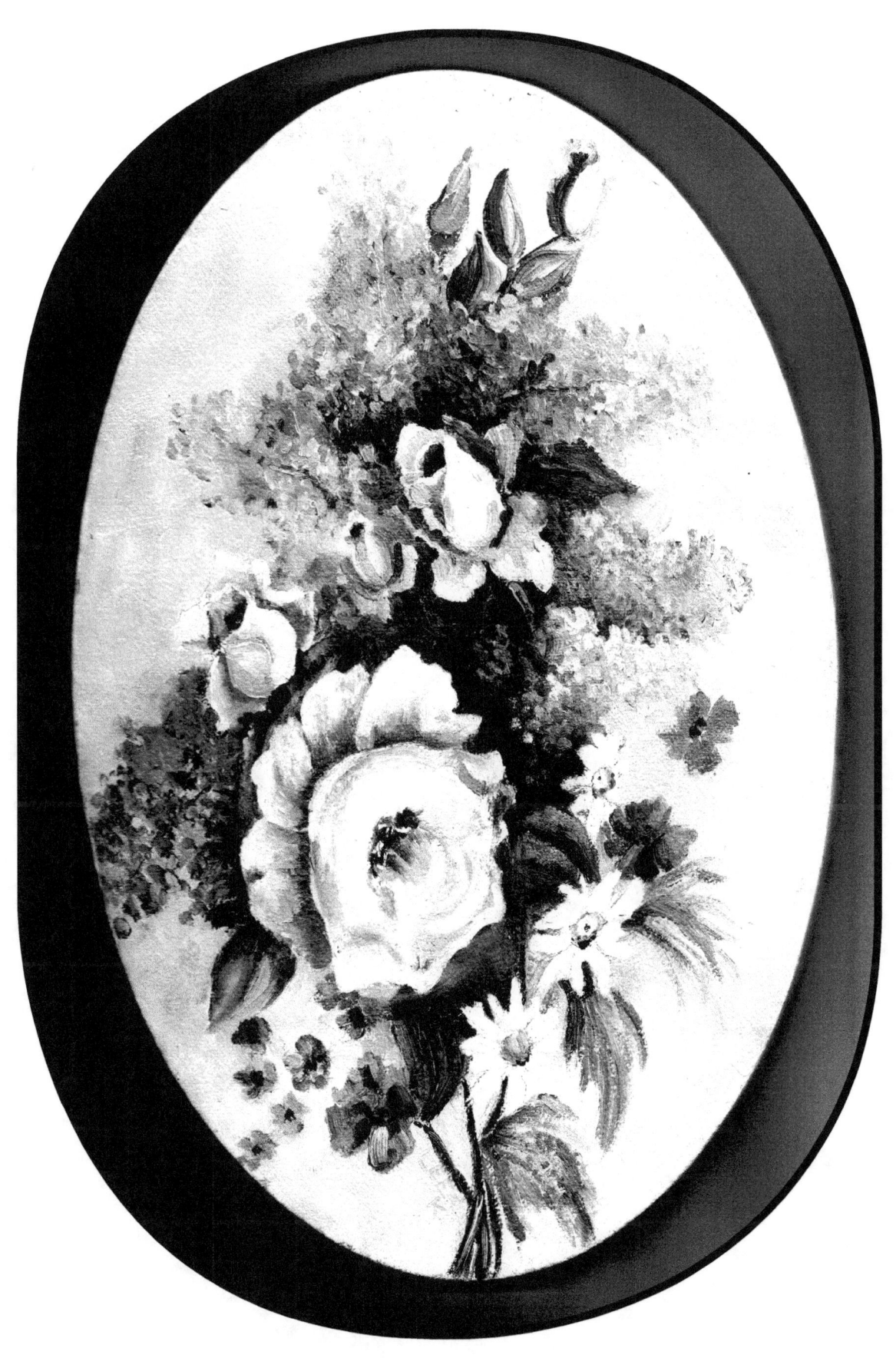

COLORING ART (COLORING BOOK FOR BIG KIDS) BOOK 1

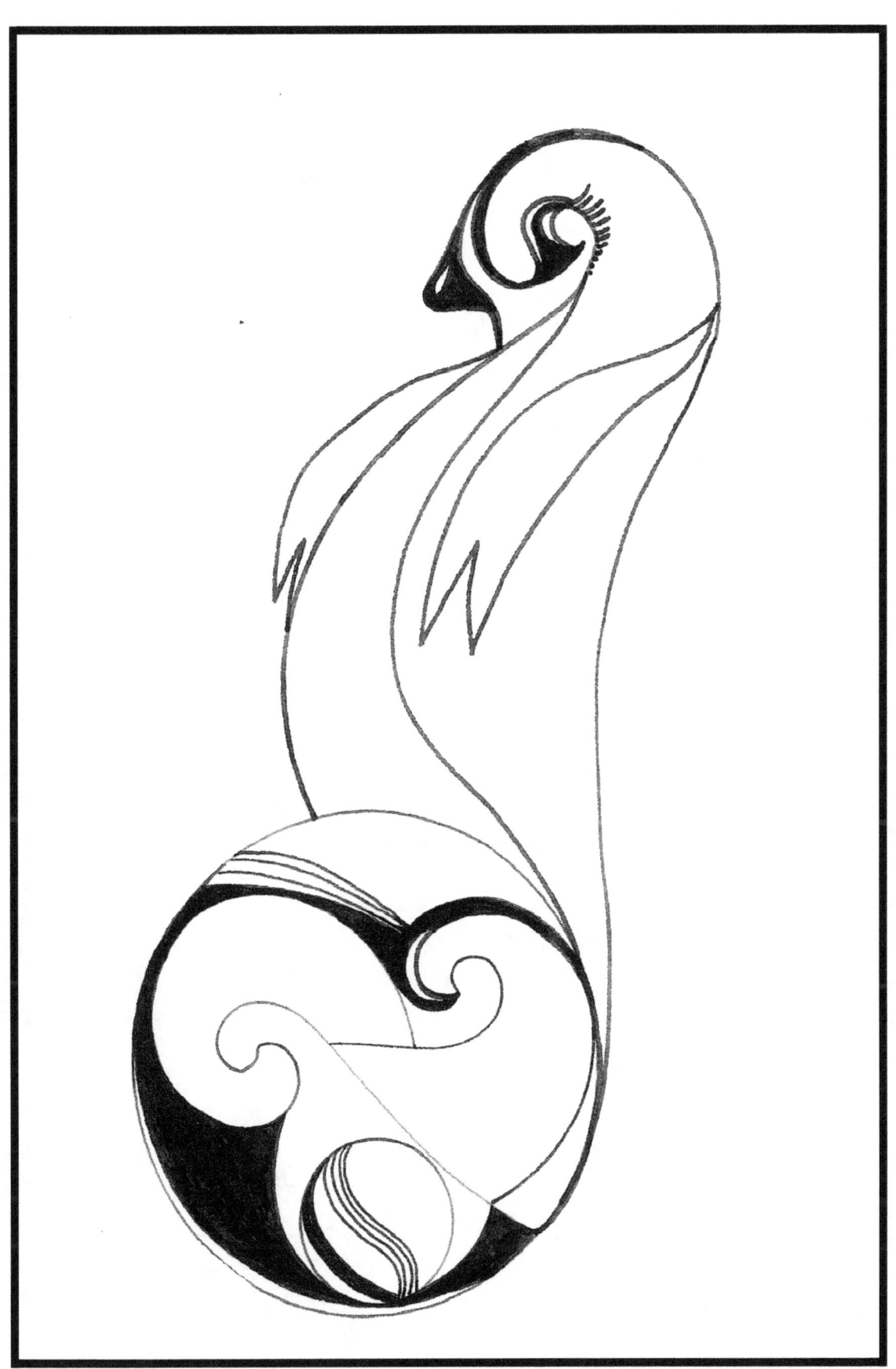

COLORING ART (COLORING BOOK FOR BIG KIDS) BOOK 1

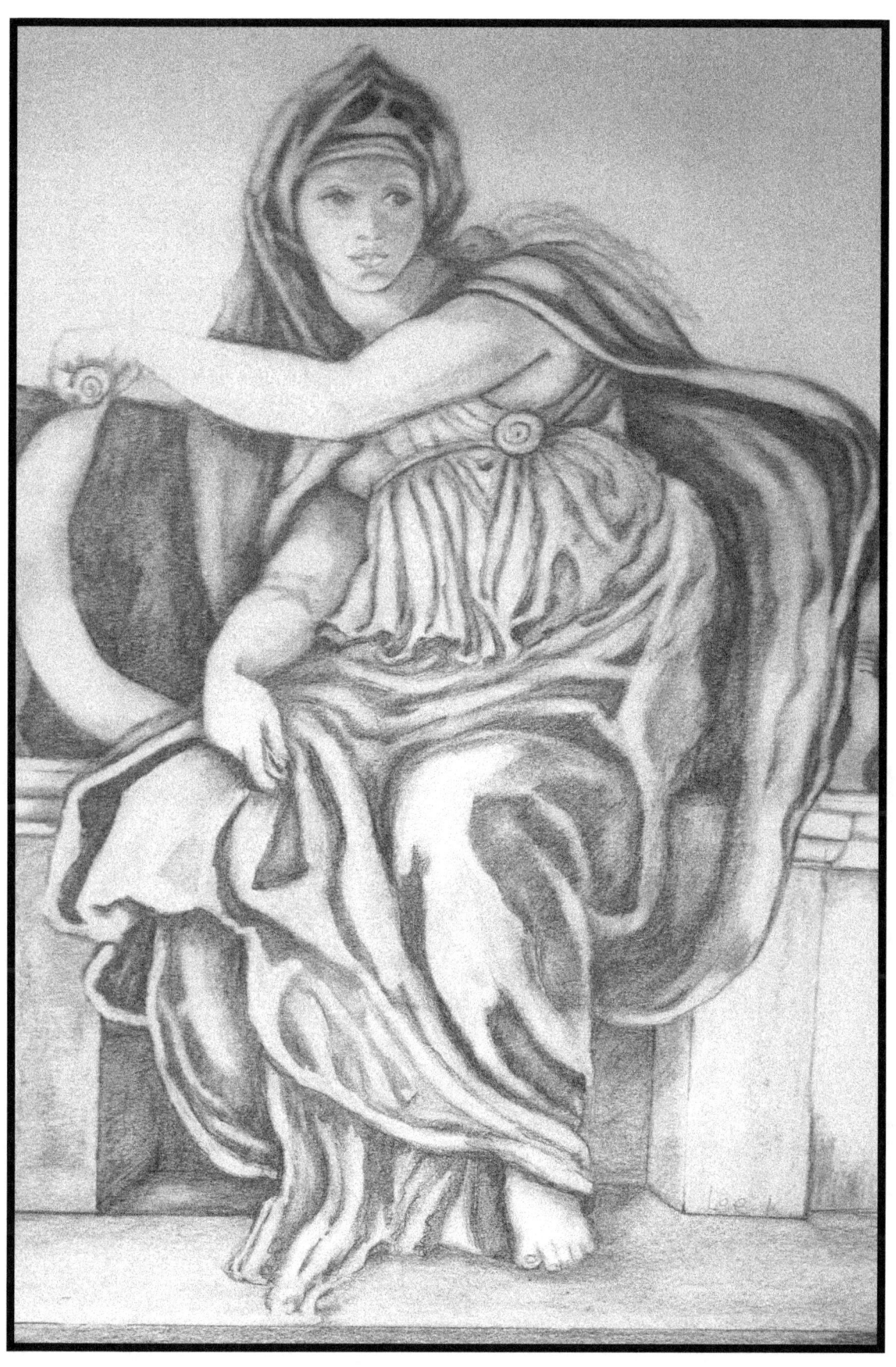

COLORING ART (COLORING BOOK FOR BIG KIDS) BOOK 1

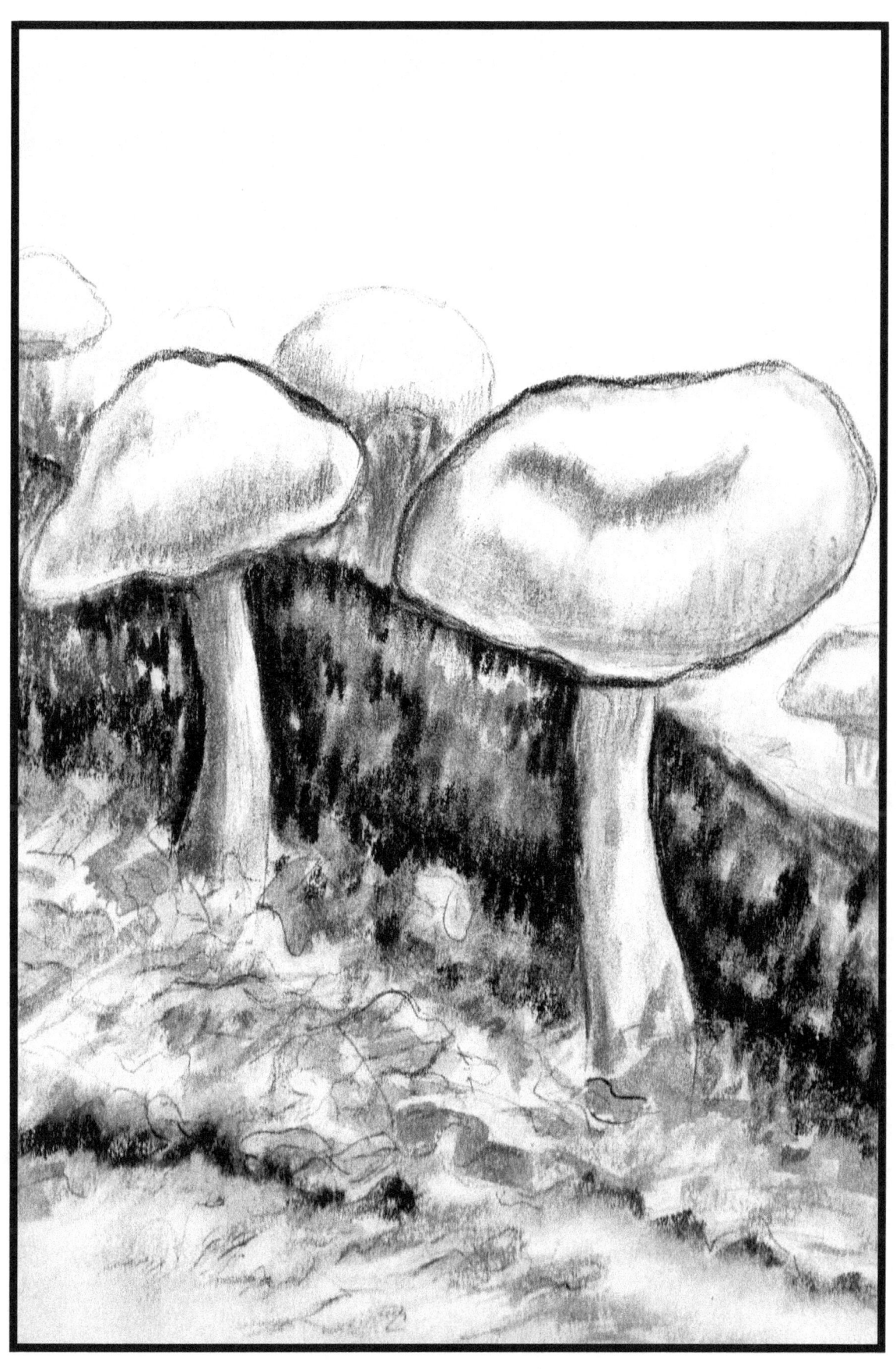

COLORING ART (COLORING BOOK FOR BIG KIDS) BOOK 1

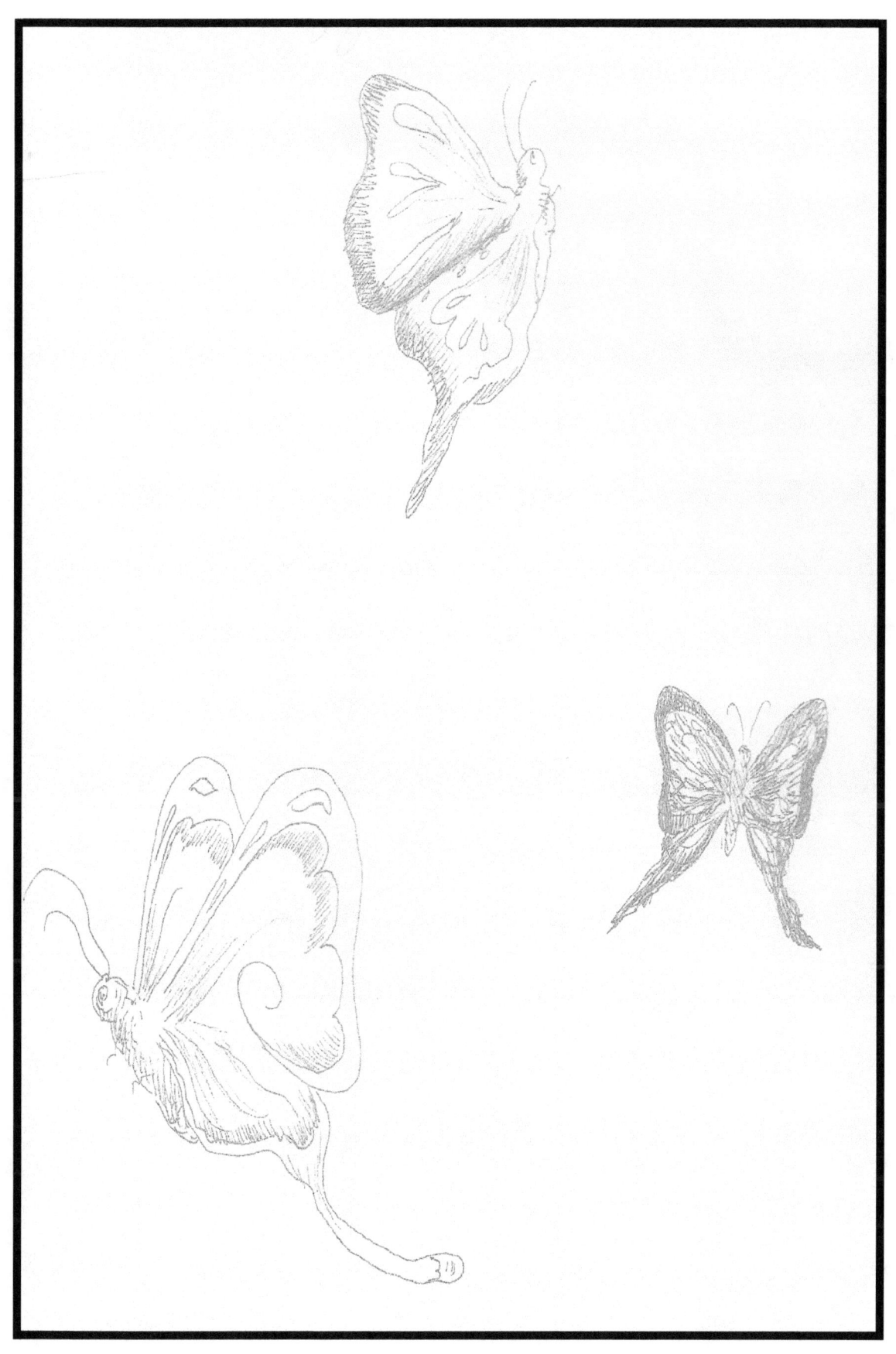

COLORING ART (COLORING BOOK FOR BIG KIDS) BOOK 1

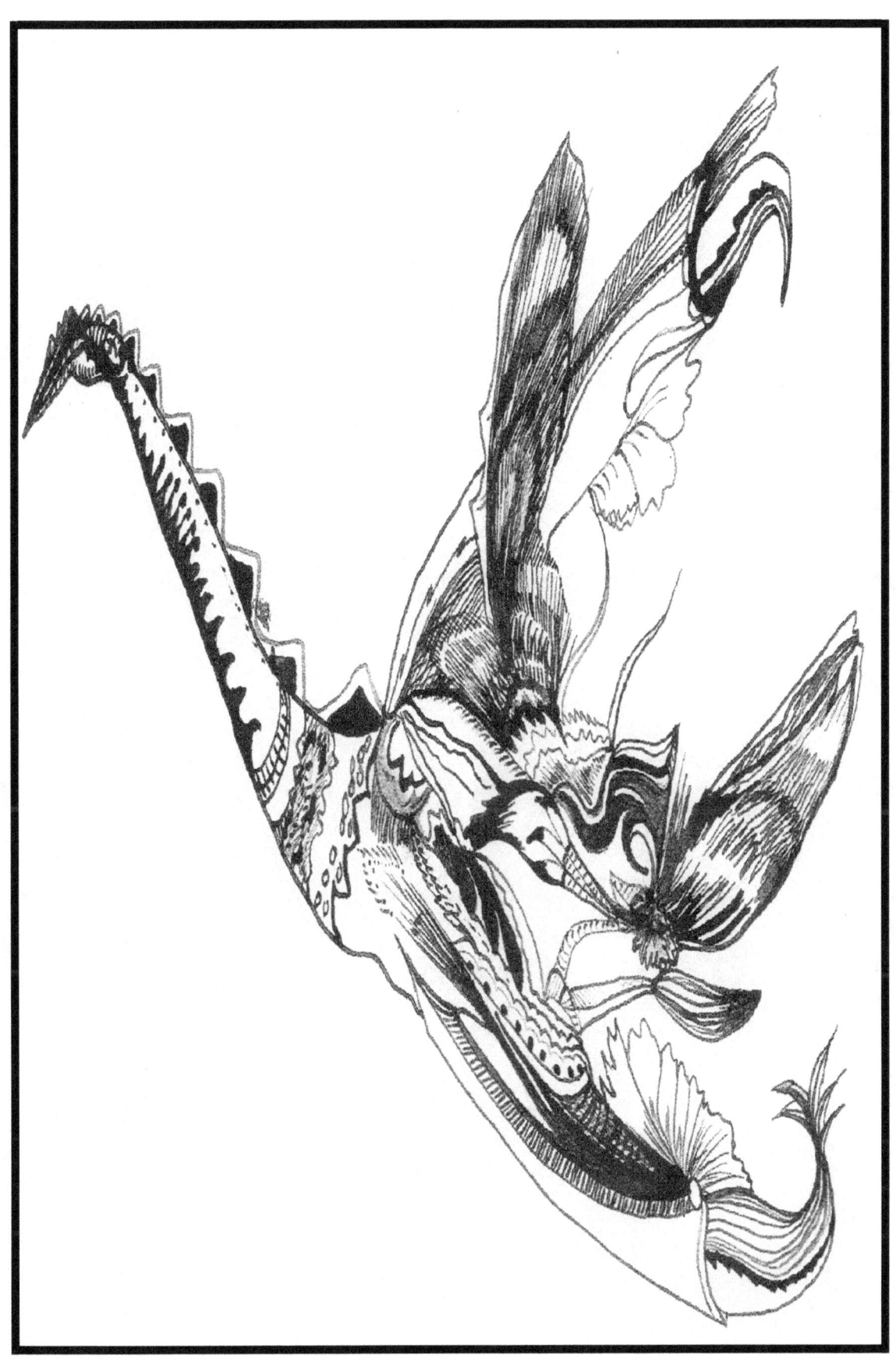

COLORING ART (COLORING BOOK FOR BIG KIDS) BOOK 1

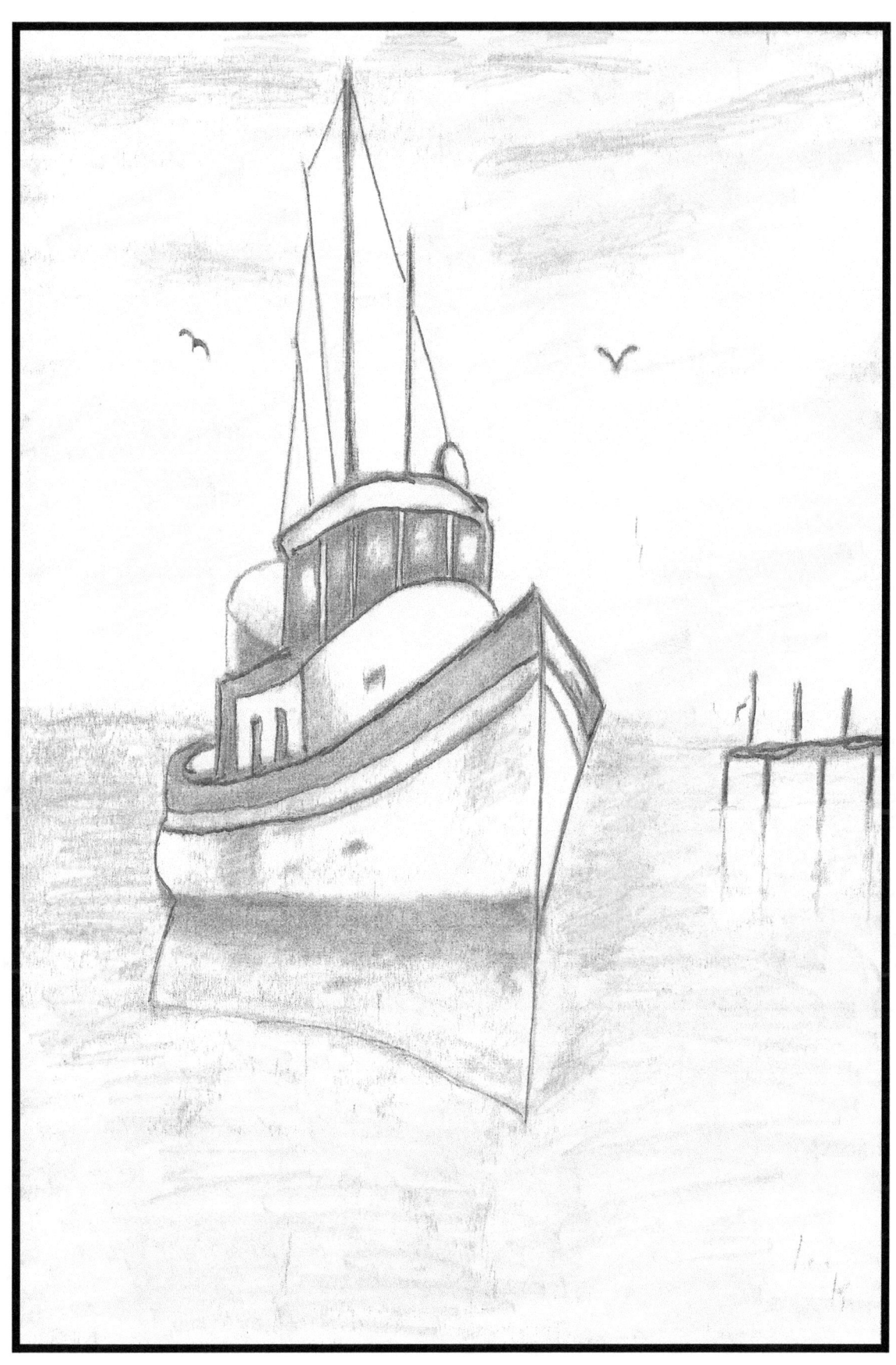

COLORING ART (COLORING BOOK FOR BIG KIDS) BOOK 1

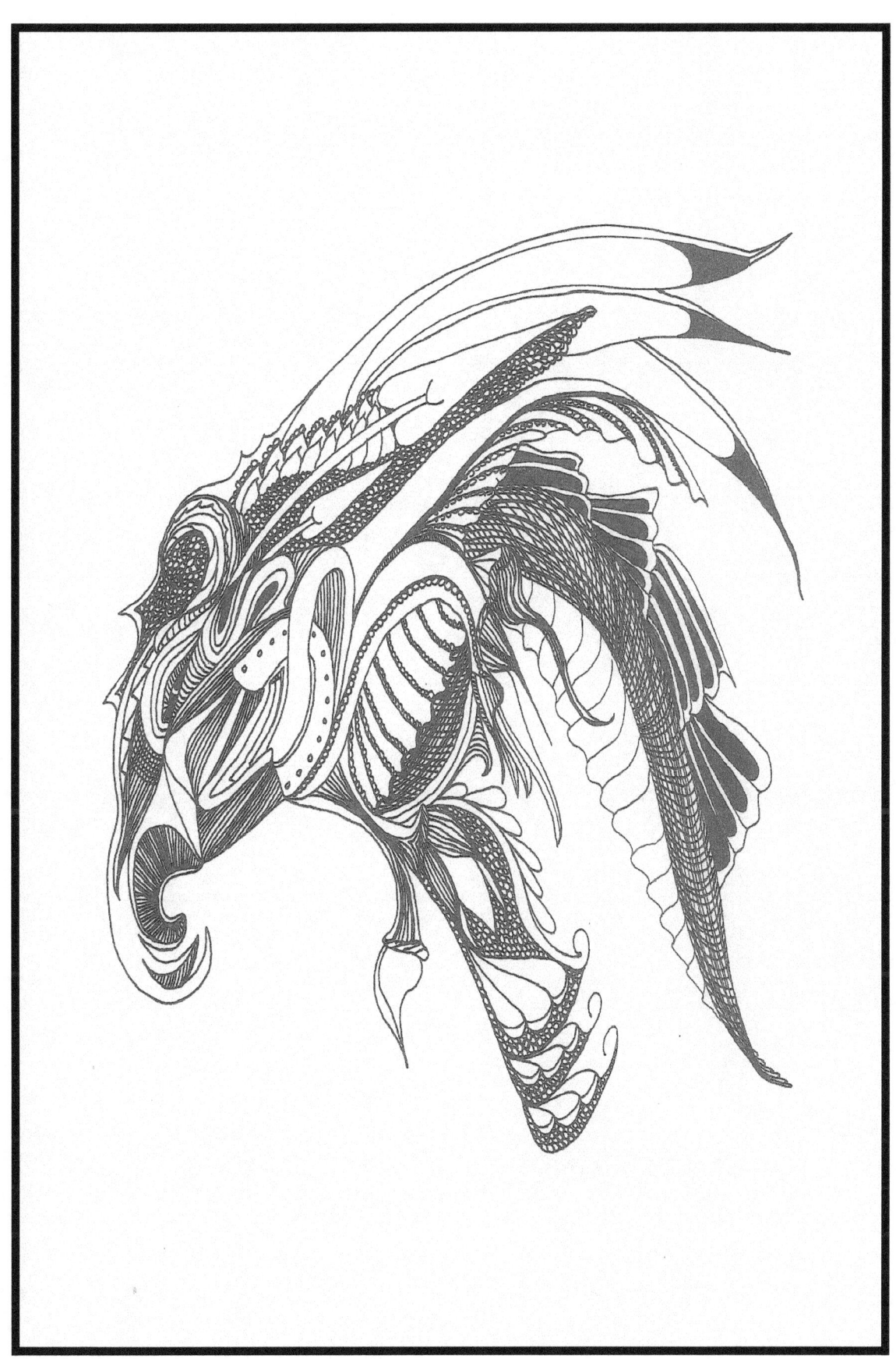

COLORING ART (COLORING BOOK FOR BIG KIDS) BOOK 1

www.ingramcontent.com/pod-product-compliance
Lightning Source LLC
Chambersburg PA
CBHW080700190526
45169CB00006B/2194